Constructing Professional Knowledge in Teaching

A NARRATIVE OF CHANGE AND DEVELOPMENT

WITHDRAWN

WITHDRAWN

Constructing Professional Knowledge in Teaching

A NARRATIVE OF CHANGE AND DEVELOPMENT

Mary Beattie

FOREWORD BY ELLIOT W. EISNER

CARL A. RUDISILL LIBRARY
LENOIR-RHYNE COLLEGE

The Ontario Institute
for Studies in Education

Teachers College
Columbia University

LB
1731
.B415
1995
Mar.1997

Published by Teachers College Press, 1234 Amsterdam Avenue, New York, NY 10027

Copyright © 1995 by Mary Beattie

All rights reserved. No part of this publication may be reproduced or transmitted in any form
or by any means, electronic or mechanical, including photocopying, or any information storage
and retrieval system, without permission from the publisher.

Grateful acknowledgment is made for permission to reprint the following:

Extracts from works by Seamus Heaney (*Station Island; The Government of the Tongue;* "Squarings
XLVI," in *Seeing Things;* and "The Stone Grinder," in *The Haw Lantern*), by permission of Faber
and Faber Ltd.

Quotation from *Four Quartets,* by T. S. Eliot, by permission of Faber and Faber Ltd. and Harcourt
Brace Jovanovich.

Quotation from *A Portrait of the Artist as a Young Man* by James Joyce. Copyright 1916 by B. W.
Huebsch, Copyright 1944 by Nora Joyce, Copyright © 1964 by the Estate of James Joyce. Used
by permission of Viking Penguin, a division of Penguin Books USA, Inc., and Jonathan Cape
(UK).

Quotations reprinted with permission of Macmillan Publishing Company from *Collected Poems of
W. B. Yeats.* Copyright 1924, 1928 by Macmillan Publishing Company, renewed 1952, 1956 by
Bertha Georgie Yeats. Copyright 1940 by Georgie Yeats, renewed 1988 by Bertha Georgie Yeats,
Michael Butler Yeats, and Anne Yeats.

Quotation from "Hen Woman" by permission Thomas Kinsella; *New Poems 1973;* Dolmen Press,
Dublin.

Quotation from *Collected Poems,* by Patrick Kavanagh, by permission of Martin, Brian, & O'Keefe
Ltd.

Library of Congress Cataloging-in-Publication Data

Beattie, Mary, 1946–

    Constructing professional knowledge in teaching : a narrative of
change and development / Mary Beattie : foreword by Elliot Eisner.

        p.   cm.

    Includes bibliographical references (p.) and index.

    ISBN 0-8077-3396-2. — ISBN 0-8077-3395-4 (pbk.)

    1. Teachers—In-service training.   2. Interaction analysis in
education.   3. Education—Biographical methods.   I. Title.

LB1731.B415   1995

371.1'46—dc20   94-38402

Canadian Cataloguing-in-Publication Data

    Beattie, Mary

        Constructing professional knowledge in teaching :
    a narrative of change and development

    Includes bibliographical references and index.
    ISBN 0-7744-0421-3

    1. Teachers—In-service training.   2. Interaction analysis
    in education.   3. Education—Biographical methods.   I. Title.

    LB1731.B43 1994   371.1'46   C95-930048-1

Printed on acid-free paper
Manufactured in the United States of America

02   01   00   99   98   97   96   95   8   7   6   5   4   3   2   1

DEDICATION

I dedicate this book to all my teachers past and present—
May what they have given to me return to them a hundredfold

CONTENTS

FOREWORD

Mary Beattie's *Constructing Professional Knowledge in Teaching* is, in many ways, an exercise in intimacy. Intimacy is not a concept that has had much saliency in research methodology. The aim of science has been to achieve an objective and dispassionate depiction of a real world. Intimacy, by contrast, is about oneself and one's relationship to another. In Beattie's terms, it is about the story through which each of ourselves is made and remade, told and re-told. That the story should figure so prominently in an effort to understand what teaching and teachers are about appears, paradoxically, both reasonable and surprising. Reasonable because stories have always been a major means through which we have come to understand how life was, might have been, or could be lived. Stories have helped us understand deep moral truths, and they have been used to condemn and convict. We have treated stories as sources of understanding and as a means of securing a true comprehension of the way things are.

At the same time, stories relate to fantasy, to imagination, to make-believe, to literature, to fiction. The idea that stories, those personally created tales about some aspect of the world, can provide illuminating and indeed dependable insights into matters as important as teaching and schooling is not an idea that fits comfortably on the dominant paradigms used in educational research. We have made, alas, a very sharp distinction between fact and fiction, and there has never been any doubt in most researchers' minds as to which is the proper category for stories.

Happily, the past decade or so has been one in which the importance of narrative, the construction of stories, and the uses of the arts in general, have been increasingly recognized for the distinctive potential contributions they can make toward understanding the personal and intimate lives that people lead. The lives that stories tell cannot be told in other ways.

What has not been much addressed is the need for artistry in the telling. Stories, after all, can be told well or poorly. Well told stories depend on the skills of the teller to craft the language, to design the plot, to exercise the imagination, and to address those nuances that keep a rider on the train so that the tale is brought culmination. Beattie's skill in storytelling is, I think, the key in sustaining the reader's interest in her prose; her Irish background and the gifts of the culture she knew as a child are easily located in her language. I believe that the acknowledgement of artistry in the kind of work that Beattie and others—such as Connelly and Clandinin, Barone, Jackson, and Elbaz—have done is of great importance. Stories, like paintings or poems or dances, are means through which a certain kind of experience can be generated. But we must not forget that the generation of such experience requires more than the use of a form of representation. It also requires the artistic treatment of that form. Stories, like paintings, can be artless. Artless work reveals little.

The importance of Beattie's work is that it extends what will hopefully become a viable tradition in the educational research community. The tradition that I speak of is one in which artistically and humanistically rooted forms of inquiry are regarded by the research community as a legitimate and illuminating means for understanding our most complex and difficult problems. To do this, we will need to understand that verification procedures that are suitable and appropriate for traditional research methods need to replaced by criteria that allow a critical reader to make defensible judgements about the credibility of the stories they read or hear. Furthermore, it will require a willingness for those steeped in more traditional methods to enter into a new and different conception of what knowledge entails. In Beattie's view, knowledge is not the discovery of facts and laws that can be nailed down once and for all, but a process that is essentially dialectic in character and enables one, through dialectical interchange, to secure what Richard Rorty calls edification. All knowledge has an unavoidable personal spin, all knowledge is tentative and constructed, all knowledge is a living process that is modified by each user. Artistically crafted narrative stimulates those processes and contributes to such edification.

Constructing Professional Knowledge in Teaching invites us into the personal life of one researcher as she collaborates with a colleague on a common journey. What results is an intimate portrait. We need intimacy in our lives—and not only in the educational research community. Beattie has given us a deep and intimate glimpse. My hope is that her work will serve as a model that will instill confidence in those who manage the gates through which young researchers must pass on their travels through academia. I would like to think that as a result of *Constructing Professional Knowledge in Teaching,* those portals will be a bit wider and faculty a bit wiser. We need good stories to help us understand; Mary Beattie has given us a very good one indeed.

Elliot W. Eisner
Stanford University

ACKNOWLEDGMENTS

The completion of this book is a joyful occasion for me and one filled with feelings of gratitude and warmth towards all those who have helped me make it possible. These voices can be heard throughout my work as they have influenced my thinking, my writing, and my life.

I will always be indebted to Anne, the teacher–participant in my study who opened her classroom, her mind, and her heart to me, and without whose generosity this book would not have been possible. Thank you, Anne, for your collaboration, your insights, your laughter, and your friendship.

I have been fortunate to work with people for whose scholarship and teaching I have so much respect and admiration. Michael Connelly's influence has been especially important in this regard. Thank you, Mick, for your pioneering work in the field, and for giving so generously of your wisdom, your knowledge, and your time during the construction of this work. You have helped me to develop my voice and to live my story as a teacher, a researcher, and a writer in new ways.

I have also had the inspiring and treasured guidance of David Hunt throughout the seven years it has taken to complete this text. Thank you, David, for teaching me the meaning of "reflexivity, responsiveness, and reciprocality." Your ideas, your voice, and your music will be with me always.

Michael Fullan's work in the field of educational change has long been an influence on me. Thank you, Michael, for your valuable direction and advice, especially at the outset of the research project, and for your insights and encouragement throughout the process.

I want to express my gratitude to Elliot Eisner, who read this manuscript with care and commented upon it with keen insight and appreciation. Thank you, Elliot, for the ideas and writings that have influenced me throughout my teaching career, and that have guided and shaped this work from the very beginning. Thank you also for your challenging and inspiring responses to the text in its various forms, and for the important contribution you made to its final form.

I want to thank all my colleagues and friends at the Joint Centre for Teacher Development (OISE/FEUT) at the Faculty of Education, University of Toronto and at the Ontario Institute for Studies in Education. The excellent seminars, discussions, and conversations we have had over the years have greatly contributed to the development of my ideas. I also wish to express my sincere thanks to Susan Liddicoat at Teachers College Press for being such a talented and thorough editor, and for making a significant contribution to the text.

My very deep gratitude goes to my husband Jim, who has given me so much support and encouragement through all the stages of this work. Thank you, Jim, for the conversations and the arguments, for the caring and understanding, for your wealth of computer knowledge, and especially for your astonishing sense of humor. Your influence and your contributions to this work sing out from every page.

CHAPTER 1

Beginning With Myself

MY OWN STORY OF TEACHING AND LEARNING

We shall not cease from exploration
And the end of all our exploring
Will be to arrive where we started
And know the place for the first time.

T. S. Eliot, Four Quartets

Prologue

These lines from Eliot have been attached to my inquiry from the beginning. I have felt the restlessness of the need to know and to explore in order to know differently. However, I did not understand my attachment to the lines until I began to accept the ambiguity of journeying backwards in order to move forward and to know that all my beginnings have held within them the seeds of their endings, which in themselves have held the seeds of new beginnings. Eliot's lines now take their place at the head of this Prologue (which is more rightly an Epilogue, in that it was written after many drafts of several chapters of this book had already been written), where they provided direction for each new phase of exploration.

The Story of the Silkie and of Narrative Unities

In May 1988, Anne Courtney and I attended the International Reading Association Conference in Toronto. Anne is a teacher and a good friend and also the participant in this research study. We went to several sessions together, one of which was about the power of story and its place in the school curriculum. The speaker told the story of "The Silkie," an old Scottish/Irish folk tale and song about the traditional belief that the souls of drowned people live on in seals who sometimes change themselves into men and come up on to the shore. They are particularly susceptible to music and will come ashore if they hear music or singing. In the shape of men, they often entice human women to marry them and go away with them. Having agreed to go, the women are then changed into seals and can never return to their friends, their families, or their homes. It is a lonely and a sad story.

Hearing it told brought waves of emotion flooding over me as feelings that had been deeply buried and long controlled made themselves felt. I felt myself responding to the beauty of the language, to the music that I alone could hear, and to the feelings and memories that the story aroused in me. I battled to keep my feelings under control and appealed to the rational side of my nature to take over and detach me from these powerful forces that were breaking loose. Tears welled up in my eyes and ran quietly down my cheeks. I tried desperately to look normal, aware of where I was, and valiantly struggled to keep this temporary "loss of control" unnoticed by those around me.

Torn between the mesmerizing effect of the ongoing narrative and the desire to turn it off in order to gain control, I became aware that Anne, who was sitting beside me, had noticed and was experiencing both confusion and concern. I noticed her quick glances, her care not to draw attention to me, her quiet knowing that something was going on but that I was coping with it in my own way. When the story finished, she leaned over, put her arm around me, and comforted me, a question flickering in her eyes and around her features. "I'm crying for myself," I answered, "for the unfulfilled part of me that I refuse to acknowledge. I'm crying for all the untold stories that are bottled up inside me, stories like this that are a part of me, that want to be written but that I refuse to write. I'm my own worst enemy, and sometimes I'm reminded of it."

I tell this story because it focuses on some of the narrative threads that link my past, present, and future together and because it brings to light some of the tensions that run beneath the surface of my personal and professional life. The narrative threads are those of the power of story, of language, of music, and of relationships in my life. Underlying these are the tensions between the emotional and the rational parts of my nature and my ongoing struggle to balance and control them. This story speaks of the tensions I feel between my active involvement in the reception of literature, music, and knowledge, and the passivity of my role in their creation. It also holds within its ending the possibility of a reconciliation and a new beginning.

I found the story painful to write. I felt again the discomfort of the embarrassing experience while I gave it a concrete form. I struggled with the urge to write it and a competing urge to bury it so that it could be dismissed and forgotten. Throughout, I wondered about the irony of my involvement in the painful process of writing a story about the suppressed pain of an avoidance of writing. I considered which pain I felt most and carried on writing.

In Seamus Heaney's (1988) description of creative writing I recognized the magnetism and the fear associated with this kind of writing for me. Heaney says that to write is to give in to that "spontaneous overflow of powerful emotions, [to respond to that] spurt of abundance from a source within [which will] spill over to irrigate the world beyond the self" (p. 13). Knowing the power of narrative to move the reader, I was also reminded of its power to disturb the balance between the emotional and the rational in the life of the writer, a balance that I have consciously constructed in my own life and work very carefully to maintain. To write narratively, the writer, who is unprotected by the objectivity and the distancing provided by other forms of writing, confronts those "powerful emotions," struggles with them for the purpose of putting them on view for "the world beyond the self," and hopes to remain unscathed. Once again, I wanted to reject narrative and to return to that comfortable, rational, objective writing style I knew I could produce without personal involvement. This, however, I knew would constitute nothing less than a betrayal of myself.

My betrayal of myself was on my mind as I listened to the story of the Silkie, and I was reminded of how, like the woman in the story, I too had left my homeland. Had it been told at that time, this story would have focused on having finished school and on choosing and embarking on a career. What it would not have described was the need I felt to develop the rational part of my nature, a part that I felt was as underdeveloped as the other was overdeveloped, a need that was strongly felt but unarticulated. This longing to see and experience the world outside Ireland, to know about the other sides of issues that had not been available to me in the course of my education, which I then perceived as too religious, too nationalistic, and too narrow, directed my choice of a new home and a setting for a career. Twenty years later, the Silkie story reminded me that I had still not reconciled these issues in my life even though I knew how to do so.

Choosing a career in teaching was quite straightforward for me, as I had wanted to be a teacher for as long as I could ever remember. I can still recall childhood games where I played the role of the teacher with great delight and the role of student with much more reluctance. I did consider and investigate several other careers, but nothing captured my imagination in the way that teaching did. The older I got, the more I understood that as a teacher I could continue my own interests in music and literature in the process of earning my living and that I could help others in the way my best teachers had helped me. I wondered about where I wanted to teach and taught for a year in Ireland before making a decision to apply to St. Paul's Teachers' College in Rugby, England. As a young, unqualified teacher in a small, rural convent school, I received a lot of assistance and support from the teachers with whom I worked. The experience reinforced my love for teaching, and I planned to teach in England for four or five years after my teacher education program before moving on to teach in other countries.

The teacher education program at St. Paul's was a three-year program that focused on both the theory and practice of teaching and learning. I chose literature and music as my major and minor subjects and consciously worked to gain an understanding of the theories behind these disciplines with an expectation that increased knowledge would help me to understand and to balance my emotional responses to them. I had grown up expecting that I would discuss and express opinions at home and in life generally but was not accustomed to these opportunities at school. As a student teacher I had a wealth of opportunities to discuss issues, to express my opinions, and to acknowledge my growing understandings. I greatly valued the three years I spent at St. Paul's, where I was provided with a wide variety of learning situations through which I felt that I gained new knowledge, new insights, and a good preparation for my life in teaching.

As a beginning teacher in a school in central London, I had my difficulties, which I understood then in terms of the impossibility of schools as places for learning. The number of students assigned to one teacher and the expectations of school administration, of parents, and of students themselves seemed to make my role an impossible one. Peripherally aware of links between students' emotional involvement with aspects of the curriculum and their interest and attitudes toward it, but within an organizational structure that I perceived as inhibiting this, I decided that in order to survive as a teacher I would have to accept what was nonnegotiable and to work within the confines of the situation to the best of my ability. Looking back at this time I can now see that the tensions between the emotional and the rational were at the heart of my difficulties. I can articulate my sense of these tensions as one of needing to bring order to my personal feelings of chaos and of needing to establish control over myself and my situation so that my classroom would be a place where creativity could flourish in spite of the organizational structures of schools. The struggle to get things "under control" was related to my sense of responsibility toward all students whose interests and emotional involvement could not be identified and fostered other than in a controlled and structured environment.

   Outside the classroom, these tensions were also present in my own continuing studies in literature, and I was consciously continuing to develop that balance between the emotional and the rational in my own understandings. I felt that I needed critical skills which would allow me to be more objective in my responses to literature, would deepen my understandings of it, and would give me the skills to respond to text with precision and control. Over the span of a 20-year teaching career, questions about the nature of teaching and learning, of creativity and control have pursued me, and I have never been able to reconcile them to my satisfaction. I now see that my efforts toward reconciliation have driven my questionings, and each new finding has led me to yet another set of questions, with each ending holding a new beginning to be explored. The process of writing a narrative dissertation was yet another journey of exploration, of the telling and retelling of the story of creativity and control as I have lived it in my personal and professional life. In writing about my response to the Silkie story, I was reminded of Robert Graves's (1975) assertion that "there is one story and one story only" (p. 137), my own story an open acknowledgment of my growing recognition that the same story has to be told and retold in each new circle of the spiral that makes up my life.

   Drawing on my experienced knowledge of teaching and learning, and on a reconstructed view of knowledge that acknowledges the indivisibility of the emotional and the rational in the act of knowing and in the act of creating, I prepared to write. I knew that in order to write narratively, I must experience and feel around me the rhythms and the sounds of my own language, music, and stories to bring out what I believe is bred in my bones. I had a strong sense of needing to revisit the place of my childhood, and by doing so, I felt again the connectedness of being in relationships with people with shared stories and shared experiences and the sense of the connectedness between the language, the stories, and the music I knew so well and the stories I would tell. I felt again the raw emotions and feelings that used to overpower me and that still have the power to do so but that I also knew were important to me as a writer. Revisiting them as an adult, I found that I could achieve a different balance and deal with their power in a new and different way, as if from "a new level of consciousness," a feeling explained to me by Heaney's (1988) use of Jung's terms to describe the development that comes about through the struggle to outgrow an insoluble conflict. My conflict would always be with me, yet I felt the development that now enabled me to be attached to the emotions and to feel their intensity, yet at the same time to be able to detach myself from them, to be capable of looking at them from many different perspectives, and to be able to deal with them through writing.

By revisiting those shared stories of which my own is a part, by feeling again the driving force of my interest in stories and their power in people's lives, and by acknowledging my own ability to control and write about it, I felt ready to bring the world of teaching and learning to light through narratives of experience. Hearing in my head Heaney's (1984) words as spoken to him by his literary ancestor, I also took them as my guide:

> ...The main thing is to write
> for the joy of it...
> Take off from here. And don't be so earnest,
> let others wear the sack-cloth and ashes.
> Let go, let fly, forget.
> You've listened long enough. Now strike your note.
> ....
> ...Keep at a tangent.
> When they make the circle wide, it's time to swim
> out on your own and fill the element
> with signatures on your own frequency,
> echo soundings, searches, probes, allurements,
> elver-gleams in the dark of the whole sea. (pp. 93–94)

Striking out on my own then, I begin with my own story, which itself begins in a childhood full of stories about the magical properties of the sea, about the land and the landscape where I lived, and about the people, the music, and the language through which I learned about myself and the world around me. It is a story of a long-term personal struggle with creativity and control and of the reconciliation of the tensions between the emotional and the rational in my life through the controlled act of creative writing. A "millstone [has] become a star" (Kavanagh, 1986), providing both light and direction for me as I begin to bring new light and insights to some of the undiscovered territory of teaching and learning:

> And you must go inland and be
> Lost in compassion's ecstasy,
> Where suffering soars in summer air
> The millstone has become a star. (p. 73)

Introduction and Flow of Events

Teachers know their classroom situations in general, social, shared ways and also in unique and personal ways. Their knowledge of teaching is multifaceted, embodied, and embedded in the narrative history of their lives, and this knowledge is practical, experiential, and shaped by the teacher's purposes and values (Elbaz, 1983). Elbaz's study is an acknowledgment of teaching as a personal and professional activity: teachers as owners and users of vast resources of personal and professional knowledge, one component of which is crystallized in the form of images of practice (Clandinin, 1983) and of classroom practices as expressions of that knowledge.

My study is positioned within the context of studies on the nature of the "personal, practical knowledge" of teachers, a term developed by Connelly and Clandinin (1988) and "designed to capture the idea of experience in a way that allows us to talk about teachers as knowledgeable and knowing persons" (p. 25). Studies have focused on teacher images (Clandinin, 1986), on rules and principles (Elbaz, 1983), on personal philosophy (Kroma, 1983), and on rhythms and cycles of teaching (Clandinin & Connelly, 1986a). The purpose of this particular study is to gain an understanding of teaching and teacher learning from the teacher's perspective and to understand how the teacher's personal practical knowledge develops through narratives of experience.

The study is set within the context of a school-based inservice program that focused on curriculum reform through reflective practice and teacher growth. Within this context, I have worked collaboratively with one teacher, and the collaborative inquiry has reached into the teacher's practices, her personal and professional experiences, and the narrative unities of her life to offer a holistic and narrative way of thinking about teaching and teachers' learning. The specific task of the study is to allow the processes of teaching and teacher learning to speak for themselves and, by interpreting and making meaning of what is spoken, to gain new understandings and insights into both. The study is concerned with the temporal dimensions of practice as past and future influence the particulars of present classroom situations, and it explores the ways in which the personal practical knowledge of the teacher, a knowledge that is cognitive, emotional, moral, and aesthetic, guides and determines curriculum decisions. Schwab (1983) explains the significance of studies such as this and the necessity for researchers to describe the artistry of teaching when he says:

> Teachers will not and cannot be merely told what to do. Subject specialists have tried it. Their attempts and failures I know at first hand. Administrators have tried it. Legislators have tried it. Teachers are not, however, assembly line operators, and will not so behave. Further, they have no need, except in rare instances, to fall back on defiance as a way of not heeding. There are thousands of ingenious ways in which commands on how and what to

teach can, will, and must be modified or circumvented in the actual moments of teaching. Teachers practice an art. Moments of choice of what to do, how to do it, with whom and at what pace, arise hundreds of times a school day, and arise differently every day and with every group of students. No command or instruction can be so formulated as to control that kind of artistic judgment and behavior, with its demand for frequent, instant choices of ways to meet an ever varying situation. (p. 245)

The conceptualization of the study is "dialectical" (McKeon, 1952), thus determining the methodology, the relationship between researcher and teacher, the outcomes expected from this relationship, and the knowledge generated by the study. Anne and I have worked collaboratively to understand and interpret the meaning of classroom practice, and we have planned, taught, discussed, questioned, reflected on, and evaluated our work together. Our narrative histories have become intertwined during the research journey, and we have grown toward a mutually beneficial relationship based on "reflexivity, responsiveness, and reciprocality" (Hunt, 1987, p. 115), a relationship which enhanced the collegial learning situation we created for ourselves as we worked together.

I believe that the significance of this study lies in its ability to describe and present the construction and reconstruction of a teacher's personal practical knowledge, and to show how this knowledge, which is experiential, embodied, and based on a narrative of experience, is used to inquire, to plan, and to develop curriculum for the present and future. Narrative methods provide us with different kinds of knowledge and different ways of representing it and have the potential to bring new meaning to the experiences of change, of growth, and of professional development in a teacher's life. Such knowledge, insights, and understandings could provide new ways for thinking about preservice and inservice education for teachers and about school improvement and educational reform. A research tradition that is accessible to teachers and that nourishes teaching and teacher growth, as opposed to any version of teacher training and the technology of teaching, may be, I believe, a worthwhile and valuable contribution.

The study is presented as three interconnected stories—my story of teaching and learning, Anne's story of professional growth and development, and our story of a collaborative and collegial partnership between a consultant/researcher and teacher/participant. I am the author of all of these stories, including those which are presented in Anne's voice. Anne has authorized the words and the forms by which she has been represented throughout these chapters and has acknowledged that they represent externally the meanings and feelings that she experienced internally.

In Chapter 1, I tell my own story of teaching and learning and describe the ways in which I believe I have constructed and reconstructed my personal practical knowledge during my life. I dwell especially on the past 20 years of my life, during which I have been a teacher and a student concurrently and have been interested in issues related to teaching and learning from a number of different perspectives and within a number of different contexts.

Chapter 2 continues this story and describes the past five years, during which I was involved in the research process. The chapter focuses on the details of the thesis process, the literature that forms the backdrop to the study, the finding of a suitable methodology within which to conduct the study, and the finding of forms with which to represent the meanings uncovered.

Chapter 3 presents the context of the study and describes the school-based staff development inservice program that provides the backdrop to my study of Anne, a participant in that inservice program and the teacher/participant in my study.

Chapter 4 tells of the course of my ongoing inquiry and of my developing understandings of the relations among image, imagination, and inquiry.

Chapters 5 and 6 present Anne's inquiry through stories of practice. The reflective process, in which image and imagination were linked and within which Anne continually constructed and reconstructed her personal practical knowledge, is described. These chapters present the meaning of the making of new relations within professional practice, a meaning that Anne explained as a question of seeing things in different ways—the same things but now seen in new ways.

Chapter 7 tells the story of our collaboration throughout the two years of the study and describes the details of a collegial partnership between a consultant/researcher and a teacher/participant in a research study. Stories of collaboration and of the interaction of our narratives are told, within which lie the details of our ongoing learning and professional development.

Chapter 8, the last chapter, is one of reflection. It describes the process of completing a circle of the spiral. It is an end that is linked to the beginning; it has opened up new possibilities and a future filled with stories—stories of inquiry, of celebration, of representation, and of empowerment of self and of others. As Heaney (1987) has said in his poem, "The Stone Grinder":

> For me, it was coming full circle
> Like the ripple perfected in stillness. (p. 8)

The Childhood Influence of Story in My Life

During the 20 years of my teaching career I have been a teacher and a student concurrently. My long-term interests and experiences in teaching and in learning provide the backdrop for a study in which my role is that of researcher, collaborator, and narrator of the everyday world of teaching and of Anne's inquiry into teaching and learning. The study is a collaborative one, and I have begun by telling the story of my own development as a teacher and learner prior to the telling of Anne's story. Anne and I have worked together to understand classroom practices and the ways in which Anne makes sense of her experiences through the concept of personal practical knowledge, one component of which is crystallized in the form of images of practice. I understand and use the term *image* in the sense that it has been used in studies of personal practical knowledge and defined thus:

> Images, as components of personal practical knowledge, are the coalescence of a person's personal private and professional experience. Image is a way of organizing and reorganizing past experience, both in reflection and as the image finds expression in practice and as a perspective from which new experience is taken. Image is a personal, meta-level, organizing concept in personal practical knowledge in that it embodies a person's experience; finds expression in practice; and is the perspective from which new experience is taken. (Clandinin, 1986, p. 166)

Through narrative inquiry and story, the interests and values of the adult and the child have come together in a meaningful and satisfying way. For the purposes of this study, I begin with my own narrative history and developing knowledge, thus enabling me to read my past experiences as a text and to understand my own personal practical knowledge as the multifaceted, embodied, historical experience it is, prior to my study of Anne and her story of teaching and learning. The thesis process has been a phase in my life's journey where I have uncovered the importance of relationships, of stories, of language, and of music in my life. The process that began with the storying of my own narrative is one within which past experiences are brought forward to deal with the present, reconstructed in the light of the new context, and focused on the future, to which they bring new meanings and significance. Like the melody that is changed forever when it is heard as part of a larger work (Carr, 1986), my previous understandings of past experiences, now reconstructed, are changed forever. Acknowledging my debt to those who have helped me to learn, in this next piece I have tried to show the way in which writers such as Yeats and Heaney have shaped the way I understand my experiences and have influenced the ways in which I bring meaning to my life.

The Living and the Dead

While reading Seamus Heaney's *Station Island* (1984) in the summer of 1988, I found myself identifying very closely with the traveler in the poems, a traveler on a pilgrimage concerned with "the growth of a poet's mind." In a narrative sequence of poems, the poet journeys inward "and proceeds through a series of encounters which lead him back into the world which formed him and then forward to face the crises of the present" (cover copy). In the final poem of the sequence, Heaney meets his well-known literary ancestor who is seemingly blind and is described as "fish-cold and bony." Joyce tells him, "You've listened long enough. Now strike your note." (p. 93) Those words came home to me, too. I had read these same poems four years previously but had not felt their impact on me in the way I felt it then. I could draw strength from the poet's ability to "make world become word" and from his openness, his vulnerability, and his willingness to allow me inside his mind, his experiences, and his feelings. I found in the poems a framework within which my own un-formed but burning questions began to take shape and within which I could respond in many different ways, responding initially with a sense of wonder and gratitude and then combining that with a probing analysis for what I could discover from them about my own writing.

Later on when I read Heaney's (1988) essays on poetry and the role of the poet, the words "new levels of consciousness" (p. 17) began to re-verberate for me, and I remember connecting them finally to Yeats (1961) and to the imagery of the tower, the winding stair, and the gyres or spirals in his work. As I was in Ireland at the time, I decided to visit Yeats's tower, which was quite close by, and to experience the place which had figured so prominently in his work. I found that the winding stairway was as integral to the tower where he lived and wrote as these symbols are to his poetry.

> I declare this tower my symbol; I declare
> This winding, gyring, spiring treadmill of a stair is my ancestral stair:
> That Goldsmith and the Dean, Berkley and Burke have travelled there.
> (p. 268)

At some unidentified time thereafter, I realized that I had begun to visu-alize my life's journey as a spiral where connected circles loop above each other, bringing "new levels of consciousness" with each circle, and to understand the thesis journey as yet another circle in that spiral, the end of which is the beginning of the next. I remembered that to Yeats, life was a journey up a spiral staircase, a journey which is therefore repeti-tious and progressive, and that through this symbol he had explored the paradoxes of change and time, of growth and identity, and of madness and wisdom.

As a remembering adult, I journey backward and inward in order to reconstruct my early felt experiences, to extract from them their meanings, and to story them narratively in the light of later experiences and feelings. I have come to understand the extent to which I learned and grew through my experiences with people and with music and story such that I now see that the issues of relationships and of music and story form threads that connect the seemingly unrelated experiences of my life's journey, give meaning to my current endeavors, and guide my imagination toward new ventures. My parents, teachers, relatives, and friends were the chief story-tellers of my childhood, and looking back now, I see that it was through the stories they told that I constructed the realities of the world I lived in and could formulate the questions that probed the inconsistencies I found there. It is my early love of stories and their power to transport me imaginatively that I wish to recapture here. I want to re-create a time now, before my formal analysis and study of stories and literature, to show their impact and power in my early life, to explore the ways in which they have shaped my thoughts and interests, and to examine how these and subsequent experiences have shaped me into the person I am today.

Remembering My Childhood

I remember my childhood as a time when I was surrounded by the warmth of close relationships and by the sights and sounds of everyday village and rural life. The rhythms of my life were determined by the cycles of religion, school, and nature, and I learned about them through the stories and music that filled my life at home, at school, and in church. My father was one of a number of wonderful storytellers in my life, and when it looked like we were going to get one of his stories, my sister Geraldine and I knew enough to become silent. One of our favorite childhood games was an invented one we called the "magic carpet ride." It involved lying still with eyes closed, holding on to the string hanging from the electric light, and waiting for the narrator to begin. The "magic carpet" would whisk us up above the houses to begin another imaginary journey to who knows where? I never cared where we were going because I knew that I would love it anyway. The night wind would blow my hair back, my body would adjust itself, and my mind would made ready for wherever this lovely, lilting language would take me. Musically and rhythmically, words carried us on our way, calling up visions of fields and sleeping animals beneath us, of isolated rooftops and stone walls. There was speed and freedom and being together. Before long, rocky land-scapes would give way to lush fields, and passing over the great plain of Meath he reminded us of the long-gone Kings of Ireland, their palace at Tara now nothing but a big field and a heap of stones. Lines of school-learned poetry recalled their glorious days, and on we sped, the rhythms of the poetry and the story blending together and carrying us along. When the houses came closer together he would finally say, "Who are we going to see tonight?" and together we would call out the name of a rel-ative or friend whose windows we wanted to peep through and to get a story about their goings-on. Sometimes he would argue, "We can't go there; we've been there already this week," but we knew we'd get our way and chanted the name over and over until he gave in and speeded us on our way. Jostling together to peer through the crack in the curtains, we always saw whomever we came to see. They would be gathered round the fire talking, laughing loudly, or maybe playing cards. Sometimes they would already be in bed and fast asleep but then, knowing no bounds, we entered the secret landscapes of their dreams and wandered around inside them until the story stopped. "We have to be getting on home now before we're missed," he would say.

Language, story, and music are threads that gave form and substance to the story of my life and give a way of understanding who I am, for I can-not remember a time when I was not involved in them in some form. Here again I have tried to reconstruct my memories of my earliest experiences with them in order to understand their full significance in my adult life.

> My mother sang softly as she worked,
> I, small and eager trailed along,
> Following the tune and all the words
> The sounds and tones that made the song.
>
> I too, sang my part with nervous voice,
> A child but given an adult's role
> Over lowered heads and silent prayers
> Into words and notes I poured my soul.
>
> A cold, rural schoolhouse would come alive,
> In poems I learned of Arctic snow.
> I could feel the wind and the bitter cold
> In his voice, in the words and my need to know.
>
> (Beattie, 1993, "Teachers")

I am remembered as a child by my mother and teachers as "a terror for asking difficult and awkward questions." Not only was this habit exasperating on its own account, but it was doubly exasperating because I usually chose to ask these questions in the middle of a story, a time when other children were listening and when the adult concerned was therefore put on the spot! As explained to me quite recently by my mother and teachers, this habit was regarded as a bit of a disadvantage in an otherwise quite nice child! Looked at within the context of my inquiry, a childhood habit of asking questions in the middle of stories took on new meanings, the stories I was being told now resonating with meaning for me and bringing new complexities and richness to my interest in narrative research.

Difficult and awkward questions still figure in my adult life, where I am separated from an oral storytelling tradition but where literature plays an important role in my life and where I rely on friends and colleagues for discussions and the sharing of ideas. My choice of literature to read is often connected to the questions I am dealing with in my life, and it is here that I not only find the answers to my questions but where I also find the seeds of new questions. The experience of having childhood incidents re-storied for me by others and the subsequent re-storying in which I engage from my adult vantage point give me understandings about the frameworks in which I formulated my questions as a child and jolts of recognition as I gain understandings about how I formulate my questions now. My findings give new meaning to my understanding of Barbara Hardy's (1975) statement that narrative is a basic way of thinking and thus of organizing human experience.

Looking back now, I realize that literature was never mentioned but that stories were everywhere—in the classroom, in the church, in the songs, and in the music. Through these stories, peopled by real and imaginary characters, dramas and adventures were played out that cast light on and evoked growing understandings of real life. Plays, too, were delightful but rare occurrences. The yearly visit by a traveling repertory company brought story, drama, costume, and music together in a way that seemed to overwhelm me as a child. I can still remember the emotional intensity associated with these experiences and the impact those plays had on me. I promised myself that when I grew up I would go to a play every night of my life.

I remember the telling and retelling of stories of all kinds as stirring my imagination, and I dreamed and planned my life as stories, complete with characters, dialogue and settings. During my years at boarding school, the nuns complained to me, to my parents, and on report cards that I daydreamed too much, but daydreaming was my way of recalling incidents in order to examine them or of constructing new ones within which I would act out many possibilities and make choices between them. I remember this as a very productive time, and when things were slow in the classroom or when I was not involved in the lesson, I could always go inside my head and get involved in the scenarios that were being played out in there. As an adult storying these experiences and recalling how they acquired meaning for me as I related them to myself and to others, I am gaining new understandings of the role narrative plays in my life. I find that I, too, "dream in narrative, daydream in narrative, remember, anticipate, hope, despair, believe, doubt, plan, revise, criticize, construct, gossip, learn, hate and love by narrative" (Hardy, 1968, p. 5).

Becoming a Teacher

My early interest in language, story, and music could have led me in many different directions, some of which I considered at the time I was finishing school, but none of them held my imagination in the way that being a teacher did. I was surrounded by friends who considered the various options and available choices open to them and talked of the tensions involved in making the wrong choice. I remember feeling tensions, too, associated with feeling that I had no options, as there was only one thing that I really wanted to be, because that was what I had always wanted to be. My acceptance and success at Teachers' College became very important to me.

At Teachers' College, my life's journey took a new turn and my story of myself as a teacher began to take concrete form. I studied music and English and looked forward to teaching as a way of introducing students to what I loved and believed in and of helping them to understand and to make sense of their worlds through stories and music in the way that I had. At that time, I had an unarticulated sense of the importance of literature and story in my own development and of its power to shape my ideas, to alter my perspective, and to give me new ways of seeing things. In D. H. Lawrence's words, read sometime in my past and well remembered, I saw the connections between my personal self and the kind of English teacher I wanted to be. Lawrence had said, and I quote here from memory, "It is the way our sympathy flows and recoils that determines the flow of our lives."

During my first year as a qualified teacher in a school in inner London, I found that the complexities of teaching were far greater than I had expected them to be. I was greatly disappointed by the extent to which my students did not share my enthusiasm and love for literature and for learning! I had spent three years learning to be a teacher, and I thought of myself as a good teacher. I knew my subject matter well, I had a wide range of teaching strategies from which to choose, and I knew the various theories of learning. "Why, then, is it all so difficult and complicated?" I wondered. "Why can I not seem to get it all together?" The tensions between creativity and control were felt everywhere in my daily life, tensions that I can articulate now but that at the time were unarticulated and that I felt as an uncomfortable sense of confusion and incompetence. I was as unable to articulate the components or the nature of the confusion I was feeling, as I was unable to plan a strategy to deal with it and resolve it. I had one other colleague in the school who was also a first-year teacher, and at the end of a day we often traveled home on the bus together and talked about our experiences. We told stories of the things that had happened in our classrooms and wondered how long we could last. We laughed at ourselves, too, because neither of us really knew what to do to be the teacher she felt she could be. I gained strength and encouragement from knowing that I was not the only one with problems but that someone else was struggling to survive and hoping that things would get better as she got more used to life as a classroom teacher.

I re-story here one aspect of my life as a first-year teacher. As I look back now, I see that I could have storied Miss Doak in many different ways, but full of my own insecurities and with a strong sense of my inadequacies and vulnerability, I storied it in my own way, and I want to present this here.

Miss Doak

My grade 5 classroom was across the hall from Miss Doak's room. Miss Doak was the grade 6 teacher, and she was very strict, very solemn, and very much in control. I regarded her with awe and with some fear. When things got noisy in my room—and that did happen no matter what I did to prevent it—Miss Doak would pay us a visit. She would cross the hall and stand at my door, riveting my students with her gaze and avoiding looking in my direction. These same students, knowing that she would be their teacher in grade 6 the following year, would immediately fall silent, and a semblance of order and control would be restored to my room.

"Oh, God, here she is again," I would say to myself when I saw her looming there in my doorway. I could look at her quite openly, noting the scowling face and the glaring eye, because I knew that she never looked at me. It was almost as if I were invisible, and that suited me fine because I wanted to be invisible at times like this. I could watch and wonder and try to figure out how she got the effect she did just by stand-ing there. I wished I could get things under control like this, and each time I would make a mental note of one thing I saw her do that I would try once she left. I always wondered what she was thinking about me, as I was uselessly standing there in that spot where she was not looking. "What a hopeless case that woman is," I imagined her thinking. "What a mess she's making of the preparation of my next class. It's going to take me until Christmas next year to undo the damage I see going on here. One look from me and these kids are perfect angels, and as soon as I re-turn to my class all hell will break loose in here again. It's too bad that her class had to be across the hall from mine."

During this first year of my career as a teacher, I often felt isolated and alone. I longed to give it up and made very serious inquiries into other fields for the first time in my life. There was no support or assistance of the kind I had received when I taught as an unqualified teacher in Ireland. I also found that these inner-city students were more difficult for me to teach than the students I had taught in any of my six practice teaching ses-sions in the cities and countryside surrounding St. Paul's in Rugby or in the rural setting in which I had taught in Ireland. In my childhood and growing-up imaginings, "being a teacher" was in no way like the reality I was then experiencing. I recall feeling overwhelmed with the responsibili-ties of designing long-range plans and interesting lessons, finding re-sources, and keeping the students under control. I often felt like a failure, especially when I compared myself to Miss Doak or to any of the other ex-perienced teachers in the school. They all seemed to have control over everything that happened in their classrooms, yet I only had control over such a small part of what took place in mine. No matter how I tried what I saw Miss Doak do, it never worked for me, and things happened nearly every day in my class that I knew might be imagined in her class but that would certainly never be acted out! Her life seemed so peaceful compared to mine.

I decided that I could not begin to think of myself as successful until I "got things under control," and I set about developing the necessary strategies, trying my own ways and observing the results. I hoped that as the years went on I would somehow get things worked out and become the kind of teacher I wanted to be. A version of this hopeful imagining did in fact take place, and as I gained experience, the confusion of the first year was gradually replaced by a growing sense of my abilities to read the situ-ations, to adapt my practices accordingly, and to see myself as successful.

After five years of teaching in London, I came to Canada, where I worked as a supply teacher at all grade levels before joining the staff of a junior high school, which I viewed as traditional in outlook and where I taught students in grades 7, 8, and 9. Lessons were subject based, and the school was organized on a rotary schedule. I found it a major adjustment on my part to become accustomed to the constant movement of a rotary program and to the daily contact with approximately 150 students who came and went every 40 minutes of the day. In London I had taught in two small elementary schools where I had contact with approximately 35 students a day and where I had the kinds of relationships with students that result from shared experiences and from knowing each other as people. My classroom management skills did not work in this new situation, and this unbalanced me for a time until I worked things out in practice, trying various approaches and observing the results. I did not really understand why my new strategies were working, but I had plenty of other things to think about and I gratefully accepted my success in this area.

"Classroom management" for me then was associated with control, and when I was successful I understood it as "being in control." I have since come to understand "classroom management" in the context of relationships and acceptable classroom behavior as those behaviors present in relationships where people know and respect each other. As my relationships with students grew and strengthened, my expectations for classroom behavior and interactions were being met. What I had then thought of as my "good classroom management skills" and "being in control," I now understand as my growing understandings of relationships and my ability to make this knowledge work for me in the classroom.

Gradually, I became accustomed to my new situation, to the rhythms and cycles of a different organizational setting, to the daily contact with four times the number of students I had been used to relating to, and to a new curriculum. My confidence in my teaching ability grew, and though never free of feelings of inadequacy and vulnerability, I had a growing sense of satisfaction with the results of my teaching gained from my own observations and from feedback given by students, colleagues, and parents.

Understanding Teaching and Learning

During the years at the junior high school, I acted as an associate teacher for student teachers from the University of Toronto. Though frustrating and disheartening at times, my attempts to help them to understand the classroom situation were satisfying and fruitful for me. I became increasingly aware of some of the dimensions of my own professional knowledge, of my ability to structure the learning environment, to create a warm and controlled climate for learning, to "read" and "flex" (Hunt,

1987), and to be responsive to the interests and abilities of students. These aspects of my professional knowledge were highlighted for me against the beginning teachers' lack of abilities in these areas. I had a growing sense of my knowledge of teaching, too, as I found myself increasingly able to articulate this knowledge in order to help my student teachers.

I grew in confidence and in my perception of myself as a successful teacher. I had 10 years of teaching experience at this point, was teaching English full time, and had gained professional confidence and a sense of professional worth. I was also aware of my shortcomings in that I was not being for all my students what my best teachers had been for me. The difference between self-control linked to personal interest and the necessity for external control in the face of lack of interest was becoming increasingly obvious to me. I was aware that I had control in my classroom when students were interested in the subject matter and that I had no control over a student's personally felt interest in the material or over a student's desire to be creative. This was something that I felt my best teachers had initiated and nourished in me and that I considered to be a characteristic of a good teacher.

To my colleagues I was a successful teacher, and they saw that my classroom was well organized, that I knew the subject matter of my courses and could transmit that knowledge to the students, who subsequently did well in their examinations. It appeared to them that I should be well satisfied with my situation, a situation that looked even better when many of my students won local and national awards and prizes for their writing. I knew the difference between outside appearances of success and my own criteria for success, which I could only articulate for myself as my inability to be as good as my best teachers had been.

As the years went on, this inability grew into a dissatisfaction with teaching. I began to feel that teaching was a constant "giving out" of energy, enthusiasm, and knowledge and the ongoing "keeping of control." The course material began to seem repetitive to me and to lack the intellectual stimulation I felt when I taught these courses for the first time. I began to focus on my feelings of dissatisfaction with the organization of schools and felt that it left little space or time for the development of sustaining relationships, for the nurturing of ideas, or for the fostering of creativity in students' lives. Given the organizational structure of which I was a part and over which I had no control, I doubted my ability to immerse students in the stories and literature that would "hook" them emotionally, give them the literary techniques they needed in order to express their own ideas, and provide situations in which they could reflect on ideas. I felt particularly frustrated with the organization of time, with the division of the school curriculum into discrete subjects, each with its own values and expectations, and with the constant emphasis on grades and marks. When I talked to students about their lack of enthusiasm for anything that was not for marks, they told me about the amount of work required of them in order to get high marks in all their other school subjects and the lack of time available for anything that was "extra." I found stories like these dispiriting, and I became involved at the school and board levels in trying to do something about the situation, which I perceived to be anti-educational.

These feelings of decreased satisfaction in my teaching life were counterbalanced by the feelings of satisfaction I was getting from the learning I was doing outside the classroom. I was enrolled in an M.A. program in English at York University, and this and my own reading gave me the intellectual satisfaction I needed but was not finding in teaching. This seemed a reasonable compromise to me at the time, and when thoughts of leaving the classroom suggested themselves to me, I was quick to remind myself of what I loved about the classroom situation—the daily interactions with students and the emotional, moral, and social satisfactions I felt from my involvement there. I reminded myself that I could find intellectual satisfaction in many places; but in spite of my dissatisfactions, where, other than in the classroom, would I find the moral, aesthetic, and emotional meaningfulness that I valued so much?

I regarded my study of literature then both as an opportunity to continue to grow as a person and to help me to improve as a teacher. More than anything else, I felt that through literature I could understand issues from various perspectives and experience realities other than my own. It caused me to grow in my understanding of myself, my understanding of others, and my relationships with others. The M.A. program was a continuation for me of the formal studies in literature I had begun in Teachers' College and had continued uninterrupted except for the first few years of teaching. I recognized and acknowledged openly to myself the way my growing understandings of the world were being influenced by writers such as Yeats, D. H. Lawrence, Hardy, and Joyce, whose voices were so important to me and whose work I admired and respected.

I expected that my increased knowledge of literature would nourish my own creativity and would also make me a better teacher. As I look back now, I see that I understood knowledge then as something that came from outside and viewed myself as a consumer of knowledge whose role was that of listener. I compared what I wrote to the literature I admired and found myself sadly lacking. I studied literature in order to learn about life but also in order to learn about writing. I read literature now for the same reasons, and the latter is now of even greater importance to me as I experiment with narrative styles to give voice to teachers' stories and try to express the felt qualities of teaching and learning.

The issues of teaching and learning took on a new perspective for me during the winter of 1980, during which I was a participant in a board in-service course taught by John McInnes, a professor at the Ontario Institute for Studies in Education (OISE). Even now, I can vividly recall the details of the situation when John showed us a piece of writing called "The Magic Butterfly" written by Jennifer, age 6, and pointed out how young children, unschooled in the formal techniques of literature, can sometimes achieve the effects of published authors and appear to do so unconsciously. I remember being very touched by the story and surprised that I was responding in this way to a story written by a 6-year-old child. Together, we talked about what Jennifer had achieved as a story writer, and we went on to identify the "literary characteristics" of her story. I began to understand how some children "know" about story through the stories they have heard and read, a "knowing" is not sought out consciously but is absorbed from contact with oral storytelling and written stories read and heard. I began to see how a very young child could be involved in the act of writing as the ongoing search for meaning and that this act has no prerequisite courses in literary theory or technique. The experience was to affect my view of knowledge, of literature, of writing, of teaching, and of my role as a teacher. I have tried to give the sense of the impact of this experience on my personal and professional life through my presentation of it here.

Jennifer and the Magic Butterfly

The first thing I remember is the picture of a glorious-looking butterfly with a fat body and big, wide wings. A child was sitting on its back, and I assumed that this was Jennifer herself. The butterfly was headed toward the clouds that billowed along the top of the picture, and this scene covered at least half the page. Below the drawing lay the simple text, written in the handwriting of a young child and complete with a few misspellings. The words invited me to go with her to wherever the butterfly was taking her, and my mind made ready to go. The butterfly took Jennifer "up, up, up to a place where birds sang, colorful flowers grew and the sun shone all day." We stayed and marveled at it all until Jennifer remembered that everyone at home would be waiting for her. She hopped on the butterfly, who immediately spread his wide gossamer wings, and with the words "Take me to home," we returned to reality.

Jennifer was 6 years old and through her words and drawing she had created an imaginary landscape and taken me on a journey there. I knew at the time that this experience had been a significant one for me, but I did not fully understand why. I felt the importance of it as an emotional excitement that threw my controlled life into disarray. Responding to it would take me deeper and deeper into the tangle I was already experiencing, a tangle that I now understand as a point of narrative conflict. My professional life, where things were "under control," was about to be turned upside down, and I was excited and stimulated at the prospect of what could happen.

Two narratives had collided, my old story of myself as a teacher and my new, undeveloped, tentative story of what I might be. Driven by my imagination, I made many changes in my practice as a result of the reflections that followed that experience and that flowed from the connection I had made between literature and my teaching. I now watched and guided students where I sensed they wanted to go, following their interests and constantly looking for moments when I noticed emotional attachments. I had decided that one of my first steps was to help students to love stories and to give them experiences of being "drawn into" stories. I began to read aloud for students' enjoyment, something I had not done at the intermediate level before, and to allocate classroom time for personal reading and talk about reading. I encouraged students to read, to talk about books of their own choice, and to write daily in the reflective journals that we sometimes shared and discussed. My experience was undergoing a reordering, and I brought my new insights to bear on my classroom situation through new classroom practices. I had a growing sense of the kind of teacher I might be and of the kinds of learning that might take place in my classroom. Now, as I think about the experience and about the meanings I subsequently gained from it, I understand how it affected my understandings and changed the way I understood the teaching of literature and writing. It also changed the way I thought about teaching and learning, as well as the role of the teacher in the classroom.

Re-storied now as part of an inquiry into the development of my personal practical knowledge, this experience and its re-storying takes on new meanings. The tension between the emotional and the rational or theoretical was at the heart of the inquiry, although I did not understand or articulate it in this way at the time. Having re-storied this experience during the thesis process, I now understand the event in new ways and see that the experience which was initially an emotional one for me was followed by insights and questions that caused conflicts with my held understandings of teaching and learning. I remember how I used to recall the emotions I had experienced in order to draw from them what I needed to guide and sustain my new practices. It was during the reconstruction of this event that I also came to recognize the connections between the Jennifer story and my memories of all the stories associated with the magic carpet ride which were so important in my early life. I was surprised by the similarities in these storied events, which had taken place with a span of over 30 years between them. Following that feeling of surprise for its meanings, I became more closely aware of the interconnecting threads linking the past to the present, and I felt a renewed sense of the power of story in my own life. My father, the string, and the magic carpet had become a 6-year-old and her magic butterfly. I was still the traveler whose imagination and emotions were captivated by story and who was working out life's understandings through this "primary act of mind" (Hardy, 1968, p. 5).

During the inquiry that followed the experience, I noticed that in spite of feeling that I was in a state of enlightened confusion, teaching was becoming a learning experience for me again and I was feeling a renewed enthusiasm for my role as it took on aspects of the collaborator, the guide, and the resource person. I began to search through theoretical material to find answers to my ongoing dilemmas, and in my efforts to bring the lives of students and the life of literature closer together, I was also bringing learning and teaching together in my own life. Connecting theory and practice together so that they informed each other involved going backward and forward; feeling doubts, wonderings, and uncertainties; and experiencing the trials and errors that are all part of being a learner. I had become a co-learner, learning about myself both as a learner and as a teacher. By exposing for students the process of writing to make meaning and of responding to literature personally, I, too, began to learn from my own reading and writing processes in the school setting. My ongoing efforts to make this process meaningful and accessible to the learner were teaching me about teaching itself.

Thus began the talking and sharing of ideas about reading and writing in our lives, the breaking down of boundaries between the school curriculum and the real world, and the crumbling of the divisions between teaching and learning. The process of teaching and learning became a cyclical one in which inquiry led to personal satisfactions, which in turn generated energy and enthusiasm for further inquiry. Relationships in the classroom changed, and the locus of control shifted from me to the students themselves. As students began to recognize their own and other's ability to create and to produce knowledge, this generated the energy and the enthusiasm for further involvement. My role had changed. Students no longer saw me as the sole bearer of knowledge, of energy and enthusiasm in the classroom; and this affected the way I saw myself.

The classroom management issue took on a new perspective at this time, too, since the shift that took place in classroom relationships required different ways of dealing with situations. I understood the issue of classroom management in this new context as one of guiding and helping 35 students to identify their interests, formulate questions, and work out problems of meaning making when this way of working was very new to them and to me, too. Once again, I developed what I thought of as a new set of classroom management skills, which I now see was the development of new and more meaningful relationships with students through their ideas and the expression of those ideas. I found that it was not necessary to control those students who had found meaning in their work. As I relinquished control very gradually, I noticed that I was helping students to develop their own abilities to be self-controlled and responsible for their own learning. This was the case for the majority of students, but there were always those who did not respond and for whom I exerted external control in the interests of the learning environment and the learning of others.

One of the greatest obstacles I had to deal with was my interpretation of the students' attitude to a teacher who was also a learner. I felt that they expected me to know the answers to all their questions; otherwise, I asked myself in their voices, "What right does she have to be the teacher?" Many students did respond to my changing practices in the way I had expected, but others seemed to welcome the changes. Trying to explain my own changing understandings to students, I explained that in English there are no right answers or formulae for success, and as I did so being reminded of how for these students, English was only one subject in a curriculum where most of the others did have right answers and strategies for success. I felt like a hypocrite and imagined that the students thought I was on some wild imaginary expedition to nowhere. I also knew that I could never go back to being the kind of teacher I used to be, as I had changed too much.

In spite of the difficulties, the obstacles, and the conflicts, I felt a renewed sense of myself as a teacher and a learner and enjoyed teaching as I had never enjoyed it before. As a co-learner, I could share the processes, the anxieties, the joys, and the triumphs of learning with students. I began to recognize that I was getting back from the situation as much or more than I was putting into it. I noticed that I was taking my cues from the students, responding more directly to their needs, and feeling that I was really helping them to learn. I found great personal satisfaction in seeing students reading and writing for their own purposes and talking about themselves as readers and writers, and I drew encouragement from watching them translating their everyday experiences into literature or relating the literature they read to the circumstances of their own lives. These feelings provided me with direction and gave me that positive encouragement I needed to counteract the ongoing obstacles and the questions constantly being unearthed by the inquiry. I found that students' attitudes, too, began to change slowly when they saw that they were being evaluated for the processes of learning and experienced the success of making their own meanings. All these observations helped me to reorganize my program to reflect my new understandings, and as I grew more comfortable with doubt and uncertainty, I gradually accepted that my understanding of what it meant to be a successful teacher had undergone a radical restructuring.

Understanding Teachers' Learning

During this restructuring of my teaching, I enrolled in the M. Ed. program at OISE in order to pursue my developing ideas of teaching and learning and to gain the theoretical knowledge to support my new practices. I also hoped to get support for the design and implementation of English programs consistent with the ministry guidelines for the intermediate division. In my new role as department head of English, I was responsible for restructuring the English programs in the school to reflect current ministry guidelines for English, which at that time mandated that at least 50% of classroom time should be spent on student-initiated reading and writing. These policies were supportive of the kinds of practices that I was working out in my own classroom; I believed that, if implemented, they would make things better for students. I began to share some of my new practices with colleagues in English Department meetings; this was considered as a help by some and as an unnecessary and unwelcome pressure by others.

When I had accepted the position as department head, I viewed the position as one where I would be responsible for the rewriting of English programs in the school and for helping my colleagues to change their practices when they conflicted with ministry and board policies and directions. With a board curriculum review scheduled for the following year, the teachers in the English Department all acknowledged the necessity to begin work on our new courses and units of study as soon as possible. Our early efforts to work together were not smooth, but given the time and the resources, I knew that I could help those teachers who objected to the ministry policies to understand them in a new way by helping them to develop new practices that would fit their current practice and that they would also regard as beneficial for students. I also understood that this might not take place within a year or that it might not happen at all in some cases. As the department head, however, I felt that I was ultimately responsible, and feeling the weight of this, I explained the situation as I saw it to my colleagues. They, too, were feeling the pressures associated with the existence of a guideline that was not being implemented and with the prospect of the upcoming board review. We negotiated the division of labor associated with the task of writing up the new courses; I was to write the courses, and, individually and collaboratively, we would write the units of study. We also agreed that we would each work to adapt classroom practices according to ministry and board policies.

My dilemma was similar to the one I had faced before, when as a classroom teacher I doubted that I could provide meaningful learning experiences for students within the organizational structures over which I had no control. In that situation, I was responsible for my own program and for students' learning; as a department head I was responsible for all the English programs in the school and for the teachers' learning. Once again, I saw that circumstances did not lend themselves to real learning, which, from my own experiences as a learner and a teacher, I knew to be unpredictable and not subject to time schedules, to the pressures of necessity, or to the felt responsibilities of those in positions of leadership. Once again, I felt the tensions between creativity and control, between the emotional and the rational, tensions that were further intensified in this situation by the feelings of loyalty I had toward the principal of the school, who trusted that I would implement the policies successfully and professionally.

Looking back now, I recognize that my growing knowledge of teaching and learning was not transferred to this new situation, where the story of my ongoing struggle with creativity and control and the conflict between the rational and the emotional needed to be retold and restructured again. I saw my role as one in which my responsibilities as a department head conflicted with the need for each teacher in the department to go through the process of restructuring his or her knowledge about teaching and learning, as I had done. I responded to the situation by going back to my old storyline where in circumstances not conducive to creativity and learning, my response was to take control, as if I could impose learning from outside. Given the commonality of the issues of teaching and learning, one might well ask why the knowledge I had gained in the classroom situation was not transferred to my department situation.

My classroom story had changed over time and had included experiences such as the one associated with the Jennifer story. These experiences and subsequent reflections had overturned my way of looking at knowledge, my perceptions of teaching and learning, and my understanding of my role as a teacher. Because of these experiences, I understood myself differently and imagined what my teaching and my classroom situation might be in the light of this restructured knowledge. Having gained new understandings about the learner as a maker of his or her own meanings, I worked out ways to organize the classroom situation to facilitate this. The restructuring of my knowledge, my classroom practices, and my role as a teacher were concurrent, and theory and practice were working together dialectically in that situation (McKeon, 1952).

No such restructuring took place in my story of myself as a department head, and in the absence of experiences that would cause me to think differently, my role remained unexamined. I lived it out in the context of my old story, a story where the tensions between creativity and control, and between the rational and the emotional, often result in a victory for control and for the rational, and where the process of reconciliation is not worked out. It is an ending with which I am all too familiar but which has caused me grief and has lain felt but unarticulated until the writing of the Prologue to the thesis. Within endings such as this, unresolved tensions are buried and forgotten temporarily, but they are the seeds of future stories waiting to be lived.

Over a period of five years I did see changes in the English programs being offered in the school, and I was viewed as being successful in my attempts to bring about positive, constructive change by administrators who appreciated the difficulties and the realities of the situation. Teachers had been treated as professionals, and change had been effected in a non-threatening, nonhurtful way. Pressure for change came from outside the school in the form of the program review, teacher inservice sessions, and teacher evaluations. Changed practices were reported in each of these, but I felt that there was no real understanding behind them for teachers, and felt that they had been superficially imposed on what the teachers really believed. In spite of our newly written courses and units of study and our changed practices, the issue of change was still unresolved for me. Questions about this and about my responsibilities toward those teachers led me to the study of "curriculum implementation" and to the search for "better models of implementation" than the ones I knew of.

Understanding My Own Learning: Embarking on the Thesis Journey

I enrolled in the doctoral program at OISE and began to study models of curriculum implementation in order to understand how practicing teachers learn and grow professionally. During my time in this program, I had the opportunity to reflect on my own learning and to explore the issue of how knowledge of my own learning could help me in my work with teachers. It was a time when I wondered about my decision to take on the role of department head when I was so happy with my classroom teaching, a role that had added tension and anxiety to my life. I came to understand my decision in terms of helping others to work things out, a feeling that had been at the heart of my decision to choose teaching as a career in the first place. I had also expected that working with adults might give me personal satisfactions and joys that I had not experienced in working with children. I often recalled a small incident that had taken place during my final teaching practice at Teachers' College and that I had never forgotten. I had been visited by an outside examiner, who at the end of the day said to me: "Have you ever thought about working with adults?" At the time, I never had, but I often wondered afterwards what he meant by the remark. When I eventually did begin to work with adults and experienced the challenges and satisfactions that I had of late thought I might, I often heard his question in my head and wondered if he had known something back then that it took me 20 years to find out.

The courses and requirements of the doctoral program provided me with opportunities to look back over the previous 20 years, during which I had been a teacher and a student concurrently, and to become aware of some of the changes in my thinking that had taken place. I began to do some formal recording of my reflections, keeping track of them in a journal and in a series of thesis proposals. I began to look at my own professional development for answers to my questions and to reconstruct my own growth as a teacher and a learner. I acknowledged the value of my years of experience in the classroom, the time I spent at Teachers' College, and my studies in literature, but found that I did not value many of the professional development activities I had attended. Over the years I had also found myself becoming increasingly uncomfortable with the way teachers were treated and viewed by curriculum developers. It seemed highly inconsistent to me that workshop leaders promoted a view of the student learner as a self-motivated, self-directed problem solver at the same time as they were treating the teacher learner as a receptacle for current teaching strategies and skills.

This attitude toward teacher learning gave very little credit to our individuality as teachers, our different backgrounds, and our different levels of experience and knowledge. I knew that most inservice programs had not helped me to develop as a professional any more than my exhortations to make learning more student-centered had helped my colleagues in the English Department. Later on when I read Marris (1974), his words helped me to understand my own inquiry:

No one can solve the crisis of reintegration on behalf of another. Every attempt to pre-empt conflict, argument and protest by rational planning, can only be abortive: however reasonable the proposed changes, the process of implementing them must still allow the impulse of rejection to play itself out. When those who have power to manipulate changes act as if they have ... only to explain, and when their explanations are not at once accepted, shrug off opposition as ignorance or prejudice, they express a profound contempt for the meaning of lives other than their own.

For the reformers have already assimilated these changes to their purposes, and worked out a reformulation which makes sense to them, perhaps through months or years of analysis and debate. If they deny others the chance to do the same, they treat them as puppets dangling by the threads of their own conceptions. (p. 155)

It was during this time that I came to understand that my growth as a person and growth as a professional were inseparable and to begin to understand this very tentatively in terms of the concept of personal practical knowledge. I tried to reconcile what I understood about student learning to my own learning and to the concept of teacher development. I read through the literature on implementation and staff development, looking for a model which focused on staff development as personal and professional growth. During the fall of 1986, I conducted a pilot study of an inservice program in writing that had the characteristic of involving teachers in their own writing as a fundamental aspect of the program. I believed that it might provide me with a concrete example of an inservice program based on teacher learning and growth. I studied the project from the perspectives of policy makers, curriculum developers, and participants and found that the teachers in this program were still viewed as adaptors of externally imposed knowledge and were being "inserviced" so that they would behave in ways concurrent with the new philosophy of teaching writing. Even though the project had the characteristic of having teachers involved in their own writing as a way to initiate reflection and inquiry into what it means to write, this project was yet another inservice program where participants are given the "official" beliefs, attitudes, and strategies about teaching. Rather than engaging in an inquiry about what it means to write and formulating their own theories of writing, the teachers were given a theory about writing and the strategies to implement it.

I felt disappointed with my findings but continued to look for a way in which teacher development, curriculum implementation, and teacher learning could be reconciled. I experienced my inability to reconcile these concepts as a major dilemma that caused me anguish, confusion, frustration, disappointment, and even rage. I eventually did untangle the threads of my confusion through discussion and argument and with the help of others, a process that led my work in a new direction and that has had a major impact on both my personal and professional life.

In this next piece, I have tried to give a sense of my attempt to work these issues out. The exchange described came at the end of a series of discussions, of arguments, of reading, and of reflection. Still tangled in the now familiar issues of control, of the emotional and the rational, I found myself up against what I could not understand. I have tried to present the situation from the two sides, showing my own attempt to grasp at meaning with a question that even I found embarrassing to ask, and the other perspective on the issue that I was eventually able to understand as a result of this experience and my reflections on it.

Chamber Music

The air in the room was filled with argument. People stood around listening to ideas singing out. Beautiful melodic lines soared, to be answered by their very counterpart. Point and counterpoint, we played.

"You're a doctoral student," he said, "you should know the full implications of what you are doing. Implementation is something you do to somebody; learning is something they do for themselves." Standing on the firm ground of what I knew, I refused to let him get away with his version of reality.

"I've been teaching long enough to know that someone has to direct how things go or else they go around and round in circles," I said. "As a department head, I have a responsibility to control what is going on in my department, so I have to find a way to help teachers to learn what I want them to know. Helping people to know, to learn, and to grow is called implementation in the school system."

"Teachers learn and grow through inquiry," he replied with emphasis on the word *inquiry*.

"What if I encourage teachers to inquire and they go in directions contrary to the department policy?" I asked.

He shook his head and the music stopped.

Standing there with half a dozen students watching and listening to the ongoing argument, I decided it was time to let her know that I'd had enough.

"I don't think I've ever met a more stubborn and argumentative woman, and she's a doctoral student, too. How long is it going to take before she understands the conflicting ideas with which she is dealing here?" I thought. This same argument has gone on for months, going around and around the same issues.

"You're a doctoral student," I told her, "you really should know the implications of what you are doing. Implementation is something that you do to somebody; learning is something they do for themselves. It's time you confronted the issue that growth and learning and implementation are conflicting concepts."

She went on then about her version of teaching and implementation, and I'd heard it all before.

"Teachers learn and grow through inquiry," I said quietly, emphasizing the word *inquiry.*

"What if I encourage teachers to inquire and they go in directions contrary to department policy?" she said.

"She's articulated her dilemma," I thought. "She needs time to think about her own question, and if she can work it through, it will be a critical phase in her journey as a learner."

Reflecting on this experience afterwards, I recalled years of family discussions and arguments and the feelings I associated with the exchange of ideas and understandings and of collaborative learning. Memories of playing in school orchestras and in a chamber music group and of singing in choirs flooded my mind, and the connections between the expression of verbal and of musical meanings began to become clearer and clearer in my mind. Remembering the deep inner satisfactions I felt during the collaborative exchange and counterexchange of musical ideas, I began to understand the social, collaborative, interactive dimensions of my own learning and to recognize the value and the power of relationships in my personal and professional life. Long afterwards, I could still hear his voice and the melody "teachers learn and grow through inquiry" playing in my mind. It returned at odd times, disturbing my thoughts and inviting me to think about it again.

During the summer of 1987 I wrote a final thesis proposal focusing on teacher development through inquiry and on images of practice during a time of planned educational change. I was returning to the school board as a curriculum consultant the following September, and one of the major aspects of my job would be to design and facilitate an inservice program for the teachers of a junior high school who were preparing for a major educational change. I hoped that one of those teachers would be willing to collaborate with me in an inquiry into the nature of the reconstruction of professional knowledge. Discussion, reading, reflection, interaction, and experience had formed another unfinished circle of the spiral for me, and I prepared to embark on my study and to move the margins of my knowing.

> All experience is an arch
> Wherethrou gleams that untravelled world
> Whose margins fade forever and forever when I move.
>
> (Tennyson, 1894, *Ulysses*, p. 95)

CHAPTER 2

Surveying the Literature

SEARCHING FOR A SUITABLE METHODOLOGY

Dust as we are, the immortal spirit grows
Like harmony in music; there is a dark
Inscrutable workmanship that reconciles
Discordant elements, makes them cling together
In one society.

Wordsworth, "The Prelude"

Setting the Scene

The purpose of this chapter is to continue the story told in Chapter 1 by telling of my developing and changing relationship with the literature that forms the backdrop to this study, within the context of the story of my life. The survey of the literature and the search for a suitable methodology for the study is a twisting, winding, looping story of my efforts to find a research context within which to describe "what actually happens in classrooms" rather than what "ought to be happening" (Jackson, 1966, p. 8) and to find forms, methods, and languages that would "describe the minor miracles of stunning teaching instead of prescribing how teachers should go about their work" (Eisner, 1988, p. 19). I have attempted to describe this experience in the next piece.

The Journey from Implementation to Inquiry

I entered the doctoral program at OISE, prepared to study the process of implementation and to design a model for the implementation of language programs that would focus on teacher learning and growth. My interest in this study resulted from my dissatisfaction with such models as I knew them, and I reviewed this literature to provide me with the knowledge and the research context for my work.

My year proceeded according to plan, but at a time when I had completed most of the required courses and had written a thesis proposal, a time when my feelings toward my work should have been positive, confident, and certain, I was experiencing doubt, uncertainty, and anxiety. These feelings grew more insistent and, refusing to be ignored, manifested themselves in a strong sense of "being in the wrong place for who I am." Pursued then by shifting attitudes toward the value of my work and by questions about the level of my commitment to the outlined study, I became increasingly aware of the significance of my dilemma and the consequences surrounding it.

Although I did not recognize it as such at the time, the experience of preparing for and writing the comprehensive examination provided the context within which I examined and came to new understandings about my research situation. One of the examination questions required me to outline a worthwhile teacher education program and then analyze what I had described within the context of two different research programs. Lines and phrases from the teacher education program I had described interrupted my thoughts for weeks afterwards, compelling me to recall the details of the answer in its entirety and to grapple with its implications. I came to see that my original thesis proposal was leading me to what Eisner (1988) referred to as prescribing how teachers should go about their work. I also came to understand that within the context of my personal and professional story, being true to myself would require me to propose a research study that would describe rather than prescribe teachers' work. I was able to resolve my dilemma and to establish a new sense of direction. In an adaptation of Wordsworth's words, I had a sense of having reconciled the "discordant elements" I was feeling, of having caused them to "cling together in one society," and of having constructed a new sense of authenticity, of coherence, and of harmony for my life.

In June 1987, having conceptualized my research question as one of knowledge, I began another draft of the thesis proposal in which I described my intention to explore the ways by which teacher learning and growth takes place through the construction and reconstruction of knowledge. I did so with trepidation but also with a sense of excitement and the expectation of harmony, knowing that I faced a new beginning.

This story illustrates the way in which my ongoing struggle with creativity and control manifested itself within the context of choosing a research framework for my work and writing a thesis proposal. It shows how theory enabled me to see how my original proposal was focused on issues of control and of controlling what teachers learned. The final proposal fo-

cused on understanding how teachers create and re-create their own professional knowledge and was based on my understandings of the distinction between inquiry and implementation. By describing my role within
two possible future stories and linking those futures with my past, I was
able to see the present from a new perspective and to choose the one that
would harmonize it with the narrative unities in my life. Retrospectively, I
can now tell this story as one of conflicting stories, and I have come to understand the dilemma as a significant one within the context of choosing
a future narrative. I tell it here because it provides the backdrop to the
story of my journey through the literature that forms the context for my
study and whose influences shaped the retelling of my narrative.

The reader will have recognized the now-familiar narrative threads,
here arranged in a fresh pattern and forming the fabric of a new story: the
tensions between control and creativity, between reason and emotion; the
importance of relationships, story, and music in my life, and the ongoing
search for a balance, a unity and a harmony in my life. Within the context
of my studies in literature with teachers such as Callaghan (1978, 1989),
Casto (1980), and Cooper-Clark (1983, 1986) who are also practicing writers and poets, I had explored the themes of relationships, memory, imagination, and ways of knowing. I had encountered these themes in the work
of authors such as Solzhenitsyn (1973), Coleridge (1974), Montague
(1972), and Wordsworth (1974) over the years, and Solzhenitsyn's words
on memory had stayed in my memory and are recalled here because of
their significance. Callaghan (1989) used Solzhenitsyn's words on the
frontispiece to his first novel: "Own only what you can always carry with
you: know languages, know countries, know people. Let memory be your
travel bag. Use your memory! It is those bitter seeds alone which might
sprout and grow someday" (p. 2). Reading them again at the same time as
I was thinking about these themes within an educational context gave me
a sense of revisiting my past and of watching it connect to the present in
ways that I knew were significant for me. By acknowledging these influences and the inherent unity of my life, understood through relationships
and the meaning-making frameworks of story, I could begin to imagine
and to construct a new and different future and bring meaning and direction to the present I was living out.

Research as Increased Self-Knowledge

The introductory story just told provides the backdrop to this chapter, which involves the changing story of myself as a researcher and my
changing views of knowledge, of teaching, and of learning. I tell the re-

search story as a story of a new beginning, a story within a story that fo-cuses on finding the music in my life through inquiry, and of the devel-opment of relationships with people and ideas that supported and nour-ished that inquiry. It is told here in the form of a personal narrative, the plotline of which loops backward several times in its journey forward, car-rying with it the questions: What is personal practical knowledge, how is it constructed and reconstructed, and how might a narrative study that fo-cuses on this best be carried out and presented? Approaching this ques-tion from a number of perspectives, I have traced my journey through the various literatures of personal practical knowledge, research methodology and narratology, then back to the former with a reconstructed knowledge of narrative as both phenomenon and method. My purpose here is to show how my knowledge was being shaped by the literature, which was in turn shaping what I read and thought, providing me with the necessary knowl-edge to conceptualize and substantiate my own inquiry.

As I now tell this research story, I am aware of the way in which my un-derstandings were reconstructed through the process of setting out such a research framework, a process that was challenging for me, required a new journey of inquiry, and resulted in feelings of personal and profes-sional growth. My study was to be a collaborative, reflective research study, set within a theory of experience where knowledge is viewed as experien-tial, as a fusion of the objective and the subjective, and where, as Polanyi (1958) explains, "within every act of knowing there enters a passionate contribution of the person knowing what is being known... as a vital com-ponent of [the] knowledge" (p. viii), and where knowing as embodied in persons, in cultures, and in the narrative unities of individuals is ac-knowledged. The process of designing the study was a situation of growth for me, "a heuristic act" that would "modify the frame of reference within which [I would] henceforth interpret [my] experience" (p. 105).

I use the concept of growth here as I have used it throughout this study and understand it in the sense that it was understood by Dewey (1916) as an "on-the-way" fruit of experiencing that is not dependent on the reaching of any predetermined goals but rather is the increasing abil-ity to resolve problematic interactions with the environment and to re-cover from loss. For Dewey growth and development involved increasing capacities to adapt and adjust to meet new conditions and new situations, and as he has explained, "there is nothing to which education is subordi-nate save more education," the role of education being therefore to create within the learner "the inclination to learn from life itself and to make the conditions of life such that all will learn in the process of living" (p. 51). As Eisner (1985b) explains, growth for Dewey "represents the extension of human intelligence, the increase of the organism's ability to secure meaning from experience and to act in ways that are instrumental to the achievement of inherently worthwhile ends" (p. 44).

My criteria for the value of education therefore, be it for others or for myself, lies in the extent to which it "creates a desire for continued growth and supplies means for making the desire effective in fact" (Dewey, 1916, p. 53). I now tell the story of my journey through the literature that supported my developing inquiry into professional learning, growth, and development and that was, to paraphrase Dewey, a journey through which my own desire for continued growth was increased and one that supplied me with some of the means by which that desire could be made effective in fact.

Journeying Through the Literature

Within the field of personal practical knowledge, I found a research perspective where I could bring together my interest in teaching and learning and in story, and I felt that I had found a research community within which I could create the kind of knowledge and meaning that I considered personally and professionally valuable. Acknowledging my debt to Elbaz (1983) and to Clandinin (1986), whose work had helped me to understand teaching and teacher learning in new ways, I began to construct ways in which I could make my contribution to the field and to extend this work with my own. The existing knowledge in this and related fields had supported my inquiry, and it now provided me with the conceptual frameworks within which I could ask my questions and begin to tell my own research story and to document my intentions in a research proposal.

I can trace my initial interest in personal practical knowledge to my tentative relationships with the ideas in this field and with the people who created them. Beginning with the ongoing work of Connelly and Clandinin (1986, 1988), I explored the existing body of knowledge and felt a strong sense of being on the periphery of something powerful. I was also filled with questions and doubts about the validity and defensibility of these ideas, yet I had a sense of wanting to understand not only the concepts but the multiplicity of implications of the findings of the research for the world as I knew it. I wanted to know how I could be authentically myself within this community and could in Heaney's (1984) words

> ...strike [my] note.
> ...and fill the element

> with signatures on [my] own frequency,
> echo-soundings, searches, probes, allurements,
> elver-gleams in the dark of the whole sea. (p. 94)

I could relate closely to the work of Enns-Connolly (1985), Elbaz (1983), Kroma (1983), and to the ongoing work of Connelly and Clandinin (1986, 1988), and felt my responses in emotional, intellectual, moral, and aesthetic ways. Exploring this and related fields, I continued to encounter the work of researchers who were new to me but who have become influential figures in my development as a learner, people such as Carr (1986), Eisner (1985a, 1985b, 1988, 1991), Hunt (1976, 1980, 1987), Johnson (1981, 1987, 1989), Polanyi (1958), Schön (1983, 1987), and Schwab (1971, 1983). In planning the inservice program for teachers within which my study would be situated, I was greatly influenced and assisted by Hunt's (1987) work. Using Hunt's idea of self-knowledge as the basis for change, I was able to conceptualize and design an inservice program that valued the experienced knowledge of teachers and within which facilitator and teachers would bring out implicit theories and beliefs about teaching and learning and thus plan our own professional growth. Between each inservice session, I would work with these teachers individually in their classrooms and would draw on these ideas and understandings.

On rereading Dewey in this context, I found a philosophical stance that supported my own theories and beliefs, causing me to wonder how much my thought had been influenced by him, whose work I had read for the first time 20 years earlier. Polanyi's (1958) ideas also supported and extended my theories and helped me frame the context within which my participant and I would engage in collaborative inquiry. I was beginning to envision a situation where the exploratory process would provide a framework for reflection and inquiry, a situation for tacit knowledge to be brought to the fore to inform current and future practice, and where the re-creation of knowledge would empower both researcher and participant. Our work together would be mutually beneficial and would be comprised of heuristic acts through which we would each learn and through the learning would "modify the frame of reference within which we [would] henceforth interpret our experience...and thus modify ourselves" (Polanyi, 1958, p. 105).

My inquiry led me to search for the meanings at the heart of personal practical knowledge research and to look for ways to identify the parameters of the field, finding the term explicated by Connelly and Clandinin (1986) in this way

The term "knowledge" points to our underlying epistemological interest and associates us with those interested in problems of knowledge and knowing in the curriculum. The term "practical" qualifies this epistemological interest by aligning us with writers such as Schön whose interest is the epistemology of practical thinking. The term "personal" qualifies our interest in the epistemology of practice by pointing to our interest in how specific individuals know their classroom situation. Accordingly, the term "personal practical knowledge" defines our interest in understanding teaching acts in terms of personalized concrete accounts of people knowing. (pp. 296–297)

As a practicing teacher, I was strongly attracted to the spirit of this research because I saw that it adopted a teacher practitioner perspective that acknowledged the teacher as a knowing, experienced professional and described a teacher's perspective similarly to Janesick's (1982) description as "a reflective, socially derived interpretation of that which the teacher encounters that then serves as a basis for the actions he or she constructs. It is a combination of beliefs and behavior continually modified by interaction" (p. 162).

The research in the field of personal practical knowledge acknowledges that teachers have a knowledge of teaching far more complex than subject-matter knowledge or knowledge of teaching techniques, and as a practicing teacher, I felt that my ways of knowing were recognized and acknowledged here. My imagination was captured by the possibilities inherent in this perspective, and I began to tell my own possible research stories, to formulate questions, and to work out various possibilities of how I might bring new meanings and new insights to the acts of teaching and learning in order to further illuminate those acts and to make a personal contribution to the improvement of education. I wrote about these feelings in a journal and expressed them in the following way:

I have a growing sense of the importance of this research. This *feels* right to me—the underlying philosophical concepts and the attitude toward teachers feels morally and professionally right. I feel a strong attachment to these ideas and to the people who are making such a contribution to the profession. This work gives me a language and a framework within which to explore the meaning of what teachers know, what I know myself as a result of my years of teaching and to find out how that knowledge is created and re-created when, as teachers, we grow in our understandings about teaching and learning, about students, classrooms, and curriculum. (July 22, 1987)

As I searched for a way in which I might conduct my research study, I focused on the literature on research methodologies and identified qualitative, ethnographic methods as best suited to my purpose. This search led me into the field of narratology, a field I had experienced previously in the context of studies in the field of language development and that I now revisited before my return to personal practical knowledge, with new understandings of narrative as both phenomenon and method. I had conceived my research question as a probe through which to explore and test hypotheses and gain deeper understanding of the issues identified rather than to produce recommendations for adoption, and I understood my choice of qualitative, ethnographic research methods as being determined by the nature of the inquiry. I believed that an action research framework (Stenhouse, 1975), where communication is symmetrical and power is equally shared between researcher and participant, would provide the basis for reflection and inquiry and would suit my research intention. My purpose was to empower both researcher and participant to bring about action and to generate knowledge by observing it, reflecting on it, and locating it within the narrative unities of the individuals involved.

McKeon's (1952) work led me to understand the need for a dialectical framework for my study in which theory and practice are viewed as inseparable and where practice is theory in action. In this view theory changes as it is influenced by action, and knowledge changes as it shifts and is restructured to meet the fluid conditions of situations. Through the reciprocal interaction of practice and theory, the essential task of the dialectic is the resolution of oppositions between practice and theory. Researcher and practitioner would collaborate to make new meanings by studying practice through a research process that is dialectical and characterized by Dwyer (1979) as "a particular form of social action that creates dialectical confrontations and produces intersubjective meanings" (p. 211).

I envisioned a study in which our collaborative findings would be presented using narrative forms. I was familiar with some of the ways in which the arts and the humanities have interpreted and described our experiences as human beings down through the centuries—literature, music, drama, history, art, and dance. I hoped to use expressive language and literary forms to describe and interpret acts of teaching and learning, and as a starting point I began to trace the theoretical underpinnings of narrative in the context of literary theory. My questions centered around the ways in which narrative studies could provide the frameworks through which practitioners' voices could be heard in the educational dialogue and within which new meanings could be brought to the human activity of teaching and learning.

My understanding of the ways in which narrative has contributed to our knowledge of the human condition was confirmed and expanded by

Kundera (1988), who explains how the great existential themes have been "unveiled, displayed and illuminated by four centuries of the novel" (p. 5). Contrary to Husserl's (1954/1970) description of the crisis of European humanity [in Heidegger's (1962) words] as "the forgetting of being," Kundera (1988) states, "If it is true that philosophy and science have forgotten about man's being, it emerges all the more plainly that with Cervantes, a great European art took shape that is nothing other than the investigation of this forgotten being" (p. 5). He goes on to explain:

> In its own way, through its own logic, the novel discovered the various dimensions of existence one by one: with Cervantes and his contemporaries, it inquires into the nature of adventure; with Richardson, it begins to examine "what happens inside," to unmask the secret life of the feelings; with Balzac, it discovers man's rootedness in history; with Flaubert, it explores the terra previously incognita of the everyday; with Tolstoy, it focuses on the intrusions of the irrational in human behavior and decisions. It probes time: the elusive past with Proust, the elusive present with Joyce. With Thomas Mann, it examines the role of the myths from the remote past that control our present actions. Et cetera, et cetera. (p. 5)

I confirmed for myself, through my readings, the way in which narrative has long been regarded as an intellectual resource in the arts, and it was in the context of literary theory (e.g. Hardy, 1968; Kermode, 1967; Ricoeur, 1984, 1985, 1988; Rosen, 1986; Scholes & Kellogg, 1966) that I had understood narrative prior to encountering the term in studies of personal practical knowledge. Hardy's (1968) and Rosen's (1986) work provided me with what I now see as the seeds of my understanding of narrative as both phenomenon and method, and these understandings were supported by the ongoing work of Connelly and Clandinin (1986, 1988), of Polkinghorne (1988), and of Carr (1986). I began to see that within the context of educational research, narrative could be used to illuminate the ways in which we understand ourselves as teachers, appraise ourselves and our experiences, and evoke and bring to life the meaning of those experiences. Hardy (1968) describes narrative as a fundamental aspect of our lives and as a primary act of mind, reminding us that "in order to really live, we make up stories about ourselves and others, about the personal as well as the social past and future" (p. 5). Rosen (1986) explains that the narrative forms we master provide us with genres for thinking with and ways to engage in the "eternal rummaging in the past" (p. 226) and in the "daring, scandalous rehearsal of scripts for the future" (p. 237).

Carr (1986) surveyed important recent views of narrative and shows how literary critics such as Mink (1978), Ricoeur (1984, 1985, 1988), and White (1973) have studied the role of narrative in history and in literature and have focused on the relationship between narrative and the events it portrays. Carr builds up a sense of narrative and experience, linking time and experience and stressing the continuity between narrative and everyday life. Showing how full-fledged storytelling arises out of life, he outlines the temporal character of experience, the key to whose structure is in its narrative character:

> The events we experience, the experiences themselves, and the actions we perform consist not of "mere" sequences but of structured and contoured sequences of temporal phases. These sequences begin and end and are thus separated from their temporal "surroundings"; and they are internally articulated in relations of suspension-resolution, departure-return, means-end, problem-solution etc. (p. 64)

Carr shows that narrative is not only the organizing principle of experiences and actions but of the self who experiences and acts. Building on the work of Husserl (1954/1970) and Heidegger (1962), who dealt with the concept of historicity, and of MacIntyre (1981), he shows the relationship between the authenticity and coherence of the individual's life and the coherence of life itself. He shows how we are "historical beings" with history serving as "the horizon and background for our everyday experiences." He goes on to explain that experience itself does not exist separately but has its own structure and parts that can be focused on separately and treated as if they were distinct, even though we experience them as parts of temporal wholes that get their meaning from the totality of the whole to which they belong. Thus, in Hardy's (1975) words, "it is nature, not art which makes us storytellers" (p. vii).

I found new understandings of the link between narrative as method and phenomenon in MacIntyre's (1981) concept of a selfhood, "a concept of a self whose unity resides in the unity of a narrative which links birth to life to death as narrative unites beginning to middle to end" (p. 205). For MacIntyre, the question of personal identity is embedded in the unity of life, the coherence of one's life story, and an individual's choice to make one kind of unity rather than another in his or her life. Personal responsibility is involved in the plots we choose for our lives, however limited, limiting, imaginative, or expansive they may be. As Carr (1986) and others have pointed out, we can choose to live our lives according to predetermined plans and narratives, or we can construct our own and choose to tell and retell our stories of who we are, what we are about, and what we are to be. Carr's words echo those of Rose (1983), who makes the claim that "all living is a creative act of greater or lesser authenticity, hindered or helped by the fictions to which we submit ourselves" (p. 17) and that "to the extent that we impose some narrative form onto our lives, each of us in the ordinary process of living is a fitful novelist, and the biographer is a literary critic" (p. 6). Heilbrun (1988) also emphasizes the power of narrative in our lives and explains that, "We can only retell and live by the stories we have read or heard. . . . Whatever their form or medium, these stories have formed us all; they are what we must use to make new fictions, new narratives" (p. 37). Looking, then, at how biography, autobiography, and narrative have all been used to study the question of how particular people are the way they came to be and the way they are, I came to realize that only narrative uses historical, emotional, personal, and factual data in an interpretative way. For my purpose, narrative alone would enable me to reveal what is meaningful for the purposes of understanding classroom practices.

My efforts to trace the research origins of personal practical knowledge had led me through narratology to the literature on teacher thinking. Reviews of this literature have been conducted by Burns (1982), Clark and Peterson (1986), Clark and Yinger (1977), and LaRocque and Oberg (1980). The latter point out that it is an indication of the newness of this field that the vast majority of the work has been done since 1976. During the past two decades, however, classroom research methods have changed considerably, and there has been a movement away from the empirical/analytical model of research, which adopts a theoretical researcher's perspective and has an emphasis on the researcher's purposes, toward that of the teacher practitioner's perspective, where purposes are collaboratively identified by the researcher and the teacher and where the emphasis is on the perspective of the practitioner. My journey through this literature led me back once again to the field of personal practical knowledge and to know narrative as both phenomenon and as method.

The research on teacher cognition began with studies conducted in the empirical/analytical research paradigm, whose purpose was to make context-free generalizations and to focus on the key issues of reliability, validity, and replication. The focus of this research was on teacher actions, on their desirable effects, and on how teacher behavior influenced student achievement. The methodology used to collect data for cognitive-process research was mainly a combination of thinking aloud protocols, stimulated recall, policy capturing, and repertory grid. Data were collected and analyzed according to frequencies of verbalizations under particular categories and relative frequencies of objectives, or activities were counted, codified, classified, and tabulated into mathematical models of teacher cognitive activity. The educational theories that resulted were valued mainly by other educational researchers, for they had little impact in practical classroom situations.

Within this field and many other fields of educational research, a recognition by educational researchers of a need for a research approach specific to education, with its own language, methods, and understanding of classroom situations, resulted in changes such as the growth of educational ethnography. Clifford Geertz (1983) has spoken of these changes as "the blurring of genres" and calls it a "sea change in our notion not so much of what knowledge is but of what it is we want to know" (p. 34). The changes have manifested themselves in a move toward what Philip Jackson (1990a) calls

> more descriptive strategies, with their heavy dependence upon narration, naturalistic observation... and an increased willingness to look and listen appreciatively to what goes on in schools, taking into account not only what is "out there" in some objective sense but also what the researcher himself contributes to what is seen. (p. 7)

The main goal of this kind of research is to observe, understand, and then provide rich descriptions of the settings observed and of the activities, beliefs, understandings, and ways of knowing of those who live out their lives in those settings. Information is collected through observation, interview, and participation, and the understandings gained, which are of the particular situational context, are expressed in the language of the situation. There is no strict adherence to scientific principles, and educational ethnographers are not concerned with maintaining detachment from the target of their inquiry but, instead, strive toward attachment and "indwelling" (Polanyi, 1958). They strive toward a description that represents the participants' world view rather than a researcher's conceptualization of teachers' personal constructs.

Research on teacher cognition expanded into several separate but interconnecting branches, one of which is that of mutual-adaptation research (Cole, 1987; Hunt, 1980, 1987). Attempting to get even closer to the situation being examined, this research position no longer accepts that observation, interview, and research-formulated descriptions are sufficient for understanding and communicating classroom practices. This branch of research views the teacher as an active participant and co-researcher; the research design, data collection, and interpretation are worked on together by the researcher and the teacher; and it is recognized that teachers hold experienced knowledge and expertise, which researchers try to understand through inquiry. It is "reflexive, responsive and reciprocal" (Hunt, 1979, 1987) in its approaches and methodologies.

Elbaz's (1983) work marked the turning point in the research on teacher thinking, as her study provided the basis for a conceptualization of a teacher's practical knowledge. Prior to Elbaz's work, the research on teacher cognition viewed knowledge as cognitive knowledge, but her work resulted in a description of the content, orientation, and structure of a teacher's practical knowledge defined in its own terms rather than in terms derived from theory. She develops the notion that practical knowledge is not just content knowledge or structure knowledge, but it is knowledge that, in Johnson's (1987) terms, arises "out of our bodily experiences and provide[s] patterns that are meaningful to us and that influence our reasoning" (p. 1).

Elbaz (1983) offers the constructs of image, practical principle, and rule to give an account of the structure of practical knowledge, and the construct of orientation is offered to define how practical knowledge is held. Five orientations of practical knowledge were identified: situational, theoretical, personal, social, and experiential. This contrasts with the view of knowledge as "fixed," "empirical," and "analytical," and it puts forward the view of the teacher as one who holds and actively uses knowledge to shape the work situation and guide the practice of teaching. I found that Elbaz's study not only cataloged the content of teachers' knowledge but also showed that teachers hold and use their knowledge in distinctive ways; and this holding and using of knowledge marks it as "practical knowledge." She worked with three major aspects of personal knowledge—its content, the way it is held (its orientations), and its structure. By demonstrating the teacher's knowledge as something dynamic, held in an active relationship to practice and used to give shape to practice, Elbaz puts forward a view of the teacher as an autonomous agent in the curriculum process.

Clandinin's (1983) work built on that of Elbaz and on the concept of image outlined by Elbaz, which had emerged from interview situations in which the teacher reflected on his or her teaching. Elbaz's concept of image did not take into account the private experience invested in an image, and Clandinin's task was to offer a conceptualization of image as a central construct for understanding a teacher's personal practical knowledge and for linking such knowledge to past experience and to ongoing practical expressions. Clandinin did this through using interviews in which a teacher expressed his or her personal practical knowledge (similar to Elbaz) and also by participating in and observing classroom practices in which routines and rhythms were also seen as expressions of the teacher's personal practical knowledge. Her study therefore reached into both the teacher's practices and the teacher's personal and professional experiences to offer a conceptualization of image.

Clandinin (1983) suggests that images are the coalescence of diverse experiences and are the perspective from which new experience is undertaken, explaining that it is through reflection that one can make conscious one's images and can set them up for inspection. Through inquiry, we can examine our own experiential history and reformulate our understanding, using image as a metalevel organizing framework that can be challenged in reflection. As Polanyi (1958) has explained: "In the act of reflection we cause our personal wisdom and experience to interact with the objective realm of knowledge to produce personal knowledge which transcends the disjunctive between 'subjective' and 'objective' (p. 300). In this way, the images we hold can be re-imagined or re-imaged, thus leading to a view of knowledge as tentative, subject to change, and progressive, rather than as something fixed, immutable, objective, and unchanging.

Through narrative inquiry, which involves a working out in practice, it is acknowledged that the teacher is a holder and user of his or her own personal practical knowledge, a knowledge that gives meaning and direction to classroom practices. It acknowledges that the curriculum situation has a past, a present, and a future that influence one another and that during inquiry, questions are asked about past and current practices, a process that is linked to the teacher's personal practical knowledge and to the narrative unities of teachers' lives. In narrative inquiry the emphasis is shifted

> from an analysis of practice in terms of theory, to a study of practice in order to develop a theory of practice but also [shifted is] the interpretative process from that of the researcher's interpretation of observed data to mutual researcher-participant reconstruction of meaning-in-action. (Connelly & Clandinin, 1986, p. 295)

This story illustrates the reconstruction of my understandings of narrative as both phenomenon and method. It shows how I came to see that through a narrative study that has the purpose of developing an understanding of the teaching process and that focuses on the meaning of classroom actions in terms of the narrative unities of the individuals, I could gain new understandings of teaching and learning as they are reflected through the past histories of participants. My future participant and I would describe, explore, clarify, and challenge our assumptions and reevaluate our practices in the light of our new experiences. The stories we would tell would capture the reflective process and the particular orderings and reorderings of prior experience in which we were engaged, showing how the threads of continuity in our personal and professional lives were being woven into a text for the present and contributing to our current views of the world. Our stories would therefore be our ways of telling who we were and who we were becoming. Through collaborative teaching, ongoing communication, and the collaborative interpretation of experience, we would mutually construct the meanings we searched for, reflect and assess our practices, and through what Dewey calls the "reconstruction of experience," we would each come to know our teaching and our practices in new ways.

Finding a Form

> God guard me from the thoughts men think
> In the mind alone,
> He that sings a lasting song,
> Thinks in a marrow-bone;
>
> (Yeats, *A Prayer for Old Age*)

Having ended my search for a research context and methodology, I still had to deal with, but continued to evade, the issue of how I would actually write up my study. This story is told in the Prologue to Chapter 1, the writing of which was the start of a new inquiry into the relationship between control and creativity in my life and into the relationship between form and content in writing. Finally acknowledging that only narrative forms could convey the kinds of meanings I envisioned, I found it was possible to imagine a study in which literary forms and expressive language could be used to illuminate aspects of teaching and learning. I began to experiment with structures and forms through which to reveal and to represent aspects of classroom life, of change and of the restructuring of personal practical knowledge. The reconciliation of form and content and of control and creativity in my life was a challenge that would bring an order and harmony to my life and that would provide "the quality of life the process of creation makes possible" (Eisner, 1985a, p. 28). As Eisner goes on to explain:

The aesthetic is not only motivated by our need for stimulation; it is also motivated by our own need to give order to our world. To form is to confer order. To confer aesthetic order upon our world is to make that world hang together, to fit, to feel right, to put things in balance, to create harmony. Such harmonies are sought in all aspects of life…(the creation of which) is a very high aesthetic achievement. (pp. 29–30)

I present here the story of my search for form, telling of the way in which a narrative researcher who stories her role as describing lives, collecting their stories, and writing narratives of storied experience attempts to live out that story in practice. My search took me back to what I knew, to the experience of centering myself and hearing my own voice, before moving forward. I have come to understand this process as one of listening in and responding to the music inside me and finding the forms with which to express it in the world outside of myself. I can best describe the process now by using a paraphrase of Heaney's (1980) words, as one of linking my roots, my reading, my reflections and my writing.

The Search for Harmony

Irish poets, learn your trade,
Sing whatever is well made,

(Yeats, *Under Ben Bulben*)

Welcome, O life! I go to encounter for the millionth time
the reality of experience and to forge in the smithy of my
soul the uncreated consciousness of my race.
(Joyce, 1922/1964, *A Portrait of the Artist as a Young Man*, p. 253)

The relationship between form and content is one that has interested artists and writers down through the centuries, many of whom have spoken of the centrality of this issue to matters of the interpretation and presentation of human experience in artistic ways. In his writing Dewey (1934) distinguishes between forms that express meaning and those that state them:

Science states meanings; art expresses them. Statement sets forth the conditions under which an experience of an object or situation may be had. It is a good, that is, effective statement in the degree in which these conditions are stated in such a way that they can be used as directions by which one may arrive at the experience.
   The poetic as distinct from the prosaic, aesthetic art as distinct from scientific, expression as distinct from statement, does something different from leading to an experience. It constitutes one. (p. 84)

Within the body of literature available to us, the variety of literary genres is evidence of the need for different modes of expression that will allow writers to produce different kinds of knowledge and to represent meanings in different ways. The work of the writer lies not in the expression of the individual's own feelings but in representing what is known about human feelings, in formulating what Langer (1957) calls "that elusive aspect of reality that is commonly taken to be amorphous and chaotic" (p. 26), and in objectifying the subjective realm. Langer explains the connection between artistic form and experience:

> Artistic form is congruent with the dynamic forms of our direct sensuous, mental and emotional life; works of art are projections of "felt life," as Henry James called it, into spatial, temporal and poetic structures. They are images of feeling, that formulate it for our cognition. What is artistically good is whatever articulates and presents feeling to our understanding. (p. 25)

Langer goes on to explain the way in which artists of all kinds create the "uncreated conscience" (Joyce, 1922/1964) of their races, their professions, and their communities through their art:

> A work of art expresses a conception of life, emotion, inward reality. But it is neither a confessional nor a frozen tantrum; it is a developed metaphor, a non-discursive symbol that articulates what is verbally ineffable—the logic of consciousness itself. (Langer, 1957, p. 26)

Like the novelist, the historian, the journalist, the biographer, and the educational researcher involved in qualitative research are all involved in the exploration of the meaning of human existence; but unlike the novelist, their subject matter is factual in nature. All have attempted to make use of the potential of language in its many forms to convey the content of human experience, and they have experimented with literary form and technique in order to do so. Sims (1984) explains that literary journalists unite the forms of journalism and literature; in order to report

> on the lives of people at work, in love, going about the normal rounds of life, they confirm that the crucial moments of everyday life contain great drama and substance. Rather than hanging about the edges of powerful institutions, literary journalists attempt to penetrate the cultures that make institutions work. (p. 3)

Kidder (1989), a literary journalist, spent a year in a classroom in Holyoke, Massachusetts, before describing the world of education for his book *Among Schoolchildren*. Kidder's narrative drew a memorable portrait of the teacher Mrs. Zajac and her students and described the daily details of classroom life, combining the personal with the professional and showing the qualitative aspects and multifaceted realities of classroom life.

Biographers and historians have also made use of literary forms and techniques in their efforts to involve both the emotions and the intellects of their readers. Using techniques such as irony, suspense, metaphor, drama, and descriptive, analytical, and narrative skills, they have tried to give readers the kinds of insights they would have had had they actually experienced the situations being described. Writing about the differences between academic and popular writers of history, Peter C. Newman (1990) explains that contemporary historians, such as Newman himself, while being true to the facts, the evidence, and the documentation, also seek to represent a truth that is "more than the sum of all the ascertainable facts" [and] "that means re-igniting the emotions of special moments—not merely recording their dates and factual details" (p. A12). Within the educational context, historians such as Fleming use the potential of language and of literary techniques in order to write about educational situations and personalities of the past, and in doing so they provide us with new understandings of our current educational situations and of ourselves. Stories of memorable educators such as Margaret Strong (Fleming & Craig, 1990) and Lottie Bowron (Fleming, Smyly, & White, 1990) help us with the telling, the living, and the retelling of our own stories within our current educational situations, and they play a part in determining the history we make and the ways in which we write ourselves into history.

Contemporary novelists such as Banville (1976, 1981, 1989), Barnes (1984, 1989), Kundera (1976, 1978, 1984, 1986, 1988), Lively (1984, 1988), McGahern (1965, 1985, 1990), and others are using form in exciting and innovative ways to explore and to present the meaning of human experience. Writing about his use of form in *The Art of the Novel*, Kundera (1988) describes himself as an "explorer of existence" and the art of the novel as the examination of new territories of existence that help us to see what we are and of what we are capable. Kundera acknowledges his debt to Herman Broch, whose revolutionary innovation was the integration of non-novelistic genres into the form of the novel. He explains that in one of his own novels, *The Book of Laughter and Forgetting*, he has used many different forms such as anecdote, autobiographical narrative, critical essay, fable, and narrative because "they illuminate and explain each other as they explore a single theme, a single question...[and] that is what holds them together" (Kundera, 1988, p. 76).

My purpose in using literary forms and expressive language is therefore to attempt to create a new form for educational research that will allow us to construct meaning in ways that evoke the qualities and feelings of the experiences being described. My hope is that these felt meanings can be represented through the writing so that a reader will come to know the realities of teaching and learning and of classroom life. I believe that such forms and techniques will bring new light to the meanings of teaching and learning and to the process of inquiry, which extends into the past, into the ways in which teachers have taught, and into the future, to the possible ways that they might teach. I believe that they will make the realities of these processes concrete, available for observation and analysis, and will allow the reader to share in, and to live vicariously within, the participant's experience.

Within each chapter, stories have shaped the meanings and the threads and the patterns within and between the stories. They have brought a sense of order, harmony, and coherence to the whole, and they have rejected any total explanation or solution concerning life because of the primary and enigmatic qualities of experience. Our descriptions have attempted to represent the realities as we knew them and the joys, the disappointments, and the surprises of the inquiry. My criteria for success has been the extent to which I felt I could enter into and understand my own world and that of my participant and could do justice to what I saw and understood through my writing. My hope is that readers will be drawn into our stories because of their coherence, plausibility, and authenticity; that they may feel their vibrations and resonances and may be invited and encouraged to tell their own stories and to raise questions about their own practices and ways of knowing. Like Peshkin (1985), I hope that my ideas, my words, and my stories will invite educators and other researchers

> to look where I did and see what I saw. My ideas are candidates for others to entertain, not necessarily as truth, let alone Truth, but as positions about the nature and meaning of a phenomenon that may fit their sensibility and shape their thinking about their own inquiries. (p. 280)

My work is located within the field of narrative studies, and the majority of the work in this field has been done by Clandinin and Connelly (1986a, 1986b, 1987, 1991, 1992) and Connelly and Clandinin (1986, 1988, 1990, 1991, 1993, 1994). In the field of educational research, narrative studies is related to Schulman's (1987) research on expert teachers, Schön's (1987) reflective practice, Reid's (1988) policy analysis, Munby's (1986) study of teacher's metaphors, Lincoln and Guba's (1985) naturalistic approach to evaluation, and to teachers' stories and stories of teachers such as those by Coles (1989), Jackson (1990b), and Paley (1981, 1986). As Connelly and Clandinin (1990) point out:

> The main claim for the use of narrative in educational research is that humans are storytelling organisms who, individually and socially, lead storied lives. Thus, the study of narrative is the study of the ways humans experience the world. This general notion translates into the view that education is the construction and reconstruction of personal and social stories; teachers and learners are storytellers and characters in their own and other's stories. (p. 2)

Within this field of narrative studies, my work has focused on issues surrounding the construction and reconstruction of professional knowledge within the context of professional and organizational change, and on the use of expressive language and literary forms to present meaning. Using the concept of interacting narratives, I show how Anne made new relations of the relations already in existence and adapted to an environment from which she had been alienated, coming to new understandings of herself and of that environment in the process. Through stories of practice, I explore the meaning of the process of change and the tensions that Anne experienced due to her inability to be responsible to those with whom she was in relation; tensions that drove her inquiry, directed her quest for increased professional knowledge and skills, and led to a reconstructed personal practical knowledge and to the enhancement of her practice. Through stories of practice, I show how Anne's desire for "high fidelity" (Noddings, 1986) drove her to increase her ability to respond and be responsive to those with whom she was in relation, and how she came to new and more significant understandings of herself, of her classroom situation, and of the community to which she belongs in the process. Through stories of practice, I show how, within interacting narratives, professional learning takes place as individuals "hold back," "reach out," listen and respond to others, enter into each other's understandings, become increasingly more responsive to shared purposes, and thus re-form themselves, their collaborative relationships, and the communities to which they belong.

CHAPTER 3

The Context of the Study

A TWO-YEAR INQUIRY INTO TEACHING AND TEACHERS' LEARNING

> And slowly answer'd Arthur from the barge:
> The old order changeth, yielding place to new,
> And God fulfils himself in many ways,
> Lest one good custom should corrupt the world.
> Tennyson, *Idylls of the King: The Passing of Arthur*

A School-Based Staff Development Program

On October 26, 1989, Anne Courtney and I co-facilitated a presentation entitled "A School-Based Staff Development Inservice for Middle School Teachers" at the first National Middle School Conference held in Toronto. As I indicated earlier, Anne is the teacher/participant in my study, and she was also a participant in the inservice program. Together we described the transition of York Valley Junior High School to York Valley Middle School and the inservice program designed to support this change. I began by telling the story from my perspective, as both consultant and researcher, outlining the inservice program I had designed and facilitated and acknowledging my debt to researchers such as Hunt (1987), Fullan (1982), Connelly and Clandinin (1986, 1988), and others whose work on teacher development had influenced me and had formed the philosophical basis on which I designed the program. I then described the collaborative work in which Anne and I had been involved during the previous two years and my longstanding interest in the ways in which teachers construct and reconstruct their professional knowledge.

Anne began her story in the year before we met and described her decision to leave her position as head of a physical education department in exchange for a core classroom position, in the year prior to the official change to middle school. Her story continued through the next two years, during which we worked together in the context of the inservice program and as collaborators in the classroom. Anne told the story from her perspective, describing her felt experiences of the change and the ways in which she learned to teach and learn in her new professional situation. The experience was a meaningful one for both of us, and when it was over, Anne laughingly said to me, "I've told you this before, but my life has never been the same since you arrived, and this is another example of it. I never imagined us doing this together." I replied that I, too, had gone into it without knowing what the outcome would be, but that I would do it all over again. Our collaborative research and all that I had learned in the process had changed my life, too, and on being invited to present an account of the inservice program, I began to imagine a presentation that would allow our individual voices to be heard as we described the story we had learned to tell together.

In our own voices, then, and using our own language and expressions, we told our individual stories and the ways in which they came together and became inextricably intertwined. By telling it this way, we felt that we invested our presentation with a richness, a depth, and a dimension that would not be possible with one voice alone. I tell the story we told here because it provides the backdrop for Anne's entry into my story of teaching and learning and for the entry of Anne's voice into my study. It tells also about the way in which we became characters in each other's narratives and the ways in which our lives met and touched each other through the interaction of narratives during collaborative research.

Sketching in the Backdrop

As a curriculum consultant, one of the major aspects of my job was to design and facilitate an inservice program to prepare the teachers of York Valley Junior High School for the transition from a junior high to a middle school. York Valley is a modern-looking, concrete building situated at the corner of a busy, major intersection in metropolitan Toronto. On three sides, the school is surrounded by concrete towers of varying sizes housing offices and apartments, and on the fourth side, it overlooks a large playing field and the bushes and trees that line the edges of the ravine. In the summertime this field is an extension of the school and is the setting for games and other outdoor activities. In the wintertime, when it is usually covered with snow, it seems to provide a wide, white, calm expanse of stillness outside that contrasts with all the color, activity, and bustle of the school inside.

The inservice sessions that I was responsible for designing and facilitating for the teachers of York Valley were focused on the assumption that knowledge about teaching and learning is, as Hunt (1987) described it, in the heads, hearts, and actions of classroom teachers. As a group of teachers and administrators, we worked together to look at our current practice, to identify ways to enhance that practice and to make it more student centered. Between inservice sessions, I worked with individual teachers in their classrooms, co-planning, co-teaching, and co-evaluating our work together. With the administrators, I worked on an official steering committee where we planned future sessions in the light of events as they unfolded as well as on a daily informal basis. I was responsible also for the coordination of visits from outside consultants, who spoke to us on issues relating to some of the organizational aspects of the middle school.

The official transition to middle school, which took place in September 1988, involved a change in both the organizational structures of the school and in the philosophical basis of the program. It involved a change in the student population of the school from grades 7, 8 and 9 to grades 6, 7 and 8 and from a program organized according to discipline-based departments to a core teaching situation with a focus on interdisciplinary learning and on student-centered learning. This required that some teachers who were accustomed to thinking in terms of subject specialization and of themselves as subject teachers had to begin to think in terms of interdisciplinary learning and the integration of concepts, skills, and attitudes across the subjects of the curriculum. The inservice therefore brought into focus the values, beliefs, images, and attitudes of the teachers themselves regarding learning and teaching and attempted to meet their stated need for support in resources, instructional strategies, and opportunities to begin to understand the changing roles of the teacher and the learner.

Both teachers and administrators were involved in a program of six full days of workshops, which took place during the year prior to and the year of the transition to middle school. Participation in the program was voluntary, as was the decision to teach in the forthcoming middle school, the alternative being to move to another junior high school in the board. I had structured many opportunities within the inservice sessions for teachers to examine their practices and to look at ways to share ideas and resources for teaching. My objective was to create learning situations in which they would look to their own teaching and to their own experiences in order to gain an understanding of that teaching, to articulate and examine their beliefs and values, to discuss them with others, to reflect on them, to evaluate them in the light of their experienced knowledge, to gain increased confidence in that knowledge, and to come to new understandings about teaching and learning. I hoped to provide teachers with experiences in which they would experience, reflect, inquire, and collaborate to make meaning of their own learning and teaching, as a result of which they would endeavour to provide similar kinds of experiences for their students in the classroom.

My emphasis throughout was on recognizing teachers as experts in their own fields and on growth through inquiry, reflection and interaction. Each session had a specific topic (described in detail in Figure 3.1) and provided time for the expression of personal opinions, reflection, interaction, and the sharing of ideas. Together we engaged in many ways to bring out our experienced knowledge, including identifying our own learning and teaching styles (Hunt, 1985), bringing out our theories of teaching (Hunt, 1980; Hunt & Gow, 1984), bringing out and sharing our metaphors and images of teaching and telling stories of our teaching (Connelly & Clandinin, 1988; Hunt, 1987) (Connelly & Clandinin, 1986, 1988).

One of the integral parts of the program was an individual project entitled "Make a Small Change." We each identified one aspect of practice where change was desired and agreed to observe, reflect on, and discuss ongoing findings with a chosen colleague. Time was allocated for the sharing of findings during each of the sessions, and it provided us with the opportunity to look at our practices, to put our actions into words, to reflect on them, and to get ongoing feedback and support from trusted colleagues.

As teachers became more comfortable with acknowledging and sharing their experienced knowledge, the time in which we spent doing this increased, and the first year of our work together culminated in a session where teachers facilitated mini-workshops for each other, answering fundamental questions of practice and helping and supporting one another. This collaboration continued on into teachers' working lives as ideas and experiences were shared on an ongoing basis, thus establishing mutually beneficial professional relationships.

The atmosphere of the workshops grew in comfort and collegiality, and some school staff who had chosen not to be involved in the inservice at the beginning of the year joined the group. The evaluations completed at the end of each workshop suggested that the participants felt good about what they were learning and felt that they were being "treated as professionals." In the new middle school, teachers would be organized in grade-level teams and their future timetables allowed for in-school planning time, thus facilitating the continuation of the sharing of ideas and resources and of collegial and collaborative professional interactions among them.

FIGURE 3.1.   A Two-Year Inservice Program for Teachers

PHASE 1—YEAR 1
1. Introduction to Teaching and Learning
    Objectives of the inservice
    Individual learning expectations
2. The Teacher as Learner
    Learning from being a learner
    Identifying and describing our own learning styles
    Learning from being a teacher
3. Instructional Strategies/The Physical Environment of the Classroom
    Learning from experience
    Sharing what we know
    A variety of instructional strategies—large group/small group/individual
4. Learning from Research: Theories of Learning and Teaching
    Learning from theorists
    Learning from other teachers/sharing our own theories of teaching
        and learning
    Learning from current research on teaching and learning
5. Observing/Record-Keeping/Evaluation/Reporting
    Learning from our students
    Learning from each other
6. Sharing our Experienced Knowledge
    Learning from our experiences and teaching each other
    Sharing our images of teaching and learning
    Ways to work together
    Evaluating our own learning

PHASE 2—YEAR 2
1. Team Building
    Working together in grade teams
    Sharing metaphors of working together
    Images of self—as learner/teacher/team member
    Images of professional growth
2. Cooperative Learning
    Cooperative learning for students
    Cooperative learning for teachers
    Images of professional growth and development
    Towards a student-centered classroom
3. Collaborative Teaching and Learning
    Learning from each other
    Learning partnerships—towards a student-centered classroom
    Images of professional growth through inquiry

An Introduction to Anne, a Participant in the Inservice Program

The inservice program provided me with the context for my study, as noted earlier, and with an introduction to Anne, who is the participant in that study. In this next story I recall the way in which I first heard about Anne and began to think about her as a possible participant. This came about through my relationship with a colleague, Carol, who was a friend of Anne's and to whom I had explained my research intentions. I hope to bring meaning to the experience known as the "negotiation of entry" here by describing it as I experienced it.

Making Connections

Sitting in the staff-room of Beech Park Junior High one morning in early September, my former colleagues and I were drinking coffee and talking about our teaching situations for the year. They were interested to know what I was doing now that I was no longer in the classroom, wondering out loud how I could possibly be busy when I had no classes to teach! I was trying to describe what it was like to work in many different classrooms and to find the time to prepare the inservice program for York Valley. I also talked about my hopes of finding a teacher there who would participate in the research I had planned. I explained that I was interested in exploring the nature of the experienced knowledge of teachers and the ways in which teachers continue to learn and to reconstruct their professional knowledge throughout their careers. I explained my need to find a teacher who would collaborate with me in this venture. "Why don't you talk to my friend Anne up there," said Carol, "I'll bet she would be interested in that. She would love to have you working with her in the classroom the way we used to work together in the gym when I was there." Carol went on to describe Anne's situation, and the more she described, the more my interest grew. She sketched out the broad outline of a teacher already involved in the process of change, an excellent teacher with whom she had worked for many years and who now needed help. I knew that I would talk to the other teachers in the school I had identified as possible research participants, and with whom I had already made appointments, but Anne sounded so perfect for me. I felt hope and excitement and the beginnings of the fear of rejection that was to grow stronger after I had met her and that was not alleviated until she agreed to work with me. That evening Carol phoned Anne to tell her that I was coming up to talk to her, and Anne told me later that among other things, Carol had said, "I think you two will really hit it off and you'll have fun together."

Before I ever met Anne, I knew a lot about her through Carol and through other colleagues who also knew her. I knew that she and Carol had worked together as physical education teachers, team teaching, co-planning, collaborating, and supporting each other. I knew that she was an experienced teacher who had planned her most recent professional change the year before and had given up the physical education headship to become a core teacher of grade 8 students. I knew that she had made this change in order to have the information necessary to make an in-formed decision about whether to teach in the middle school or to move to another junior high school when the official change took place at York Valley. When I met her, Anne had already taught for over a year in the core classroom situation, had decided to teach in the forthcoming middle school, and planned to attend the inservice sessions. She was a voluntary member of the Middle School Implementation Committee and was ac-tively involved in setting up the necessary frameworks and schedules for the new middle school. Understanding that teaching in the middle school organization would require changes in teaching methods, in classroom structures, and in subject-matter knowledge, she had already begun to pre-pare for it in her own time and at her own pace. In her first year she had participated in several new professional experiences, learned some new subject matter, and begun to try out some new teaching strategies such as learning partnerships, small-group learning, and cooperative learning.

When I met Anne, I was a newly appointed consultant and con-sciously working out for myself what it actually meant to be a consultant and to work within a consultative relationship. In the relationship with Anne, I found a situation of professional collegiality that I had never ex-perienced in my life as a classroom teacher, where I had often felt isolated and separate. In this relationship I found that I could give and receive; I could explore my own questions with a trusted and empathetic colleague and feel that I, too, could provide the support and empathy necessary for Anne's inquiry. As our relationship developed, I was conscious of the level of trust I was experiencing, enabling me to take risks I could not have imagined taking and openly exploring the tensions I felt between creativ-ity and control in this new situation. I acknowledged the feelings of pro-fessional growth I was experiencing and the sense of the development of balance and unity in my life. I talked and wrote about these issues within the context of my thesis journey and within the context of my life. In this next piece, I have tried to describe the movement from the "negotiation of entry" into the beginnings of our collaboration and of my early intimations that I had found a professional relationship within which I could be "reflexive, responsive and reciprocal" (Hunt, 1987, p. 115).

Finding a Partner

Anne agreed to think about my proposal for collaborative research, and hoping that she would accept me, I waited patiently for her reply. It came after the first inservice session. Waiting until the others had left, Anne told me that she would be happy to work with me. Her decision had come to mean a lot to me, and I felt a great sense of relief and delight. The longer I had known Anne, the more I knew that I wanted to work with her and the more important her decision became to me.

Almost immediately, we started to talk about how we would begin to work together in the classroom, acknowledging the importance of providing each other with feedback and of monitoring the benefits of the collaboration for each of us. Our schedule involved a twice-weekly session of collaborative work in the first year and a weekly session during the second year. It also included two open-ended interviews (June 1988 and November 1988), attending many school meetings and professional development sessions together, and many informal planning sessions and conversations. Our collaborative classroom work and the inservice provided Anne and me with opportunities to be a part of each other's work, to provide feedback and support, and to learn from each other. We began to see how our work together could be mutually beneficial and to talk to each other about these ways. I now had a situation in which I could examine my need for structure and organization and the tension I feel between giving learners the freedom they need to inquire and explore and the right amount of structure and support as they do so. It was the first time that I had discussed this openly with a colleague, and the feedback I received was supportive, helpful, and valuable to me, encouraging me to pursue the issues and to work out my dilemmas. I understood my challenge as one of allowing teachers to control their own learning and my role as one of facilitating learning and of providing the necessary freedom and support. I concentrated on achieving a balance between providing the information and specific skills that teachers wanted and the time and situations necessary for ongoing interaction, reflection, and inquiry.

The tension between freedom and control was a constant source of discussion for Anne and me, as we perceived that we both felt the same tension in our differing roles as inservice facilitator and classroom teacher. We talked about our mutual recognition of the need for learners to have freedom to learn, and we both felt that total freedom without structure or support would be an abdication of responsibility on the part of the teacher. We were able to talk about our shared understandings of the ways in which learning is facilitated in situations where the learner feels responsible and in control and to discuss ways of providing those situations without abdicating responsibility. Because of our roles within each other's situations, we were able to understand those situations in unique ways and to provide valuable support and feedback.

As I retell this story now, I recognize that the experience of designing and facilitating the inservice program, together with the intensive participant observation schedule, was a rich learning experience for me. My situation was one in which my research and my professional work were deeply intertwined and in which one supported and nourished the other. I was engaged in an ongoing cycle of practice, reflection, formulation, and reformulation of theories about teaching and learning where theory and practice were juxtaposed and where I focused on working out oppositions in theory and practice during reflection on and examinations of practice. My understanding of theory was deepened as I observed how it was created for me through reflective practice, and my practices changed as a result of the interaction of theory and practice and the ongoing reconstruction of my personal practical knowledge.

I learned personally and professionally through my efforts to focus on understanding Anne's teaching from her perspective. I gained insights that threaded themselves into many areas of both my professional and personal life, helping me with my efforts to be more empathetic and understanding of the people in my life and less judgmental of them. In my work with Anne, I also focused on my desire to be a better listener and began to feel that the work I was doing was about everything that was important to me. I had a growing sense of harmony and unity that came from seeing the relatedness of the personal and professional aspects of my life and from the sense that Anne and I were both growing professionally because of our collaboration. As the inservice progressed, I developed increasing confidence in my ability to facilitate teachers' learning and to focus on an "inside-out" (Hunt, 1987) approach. This was because of the positive feedback I received from the teachers after each of the sessions and also because I was experiencing in my relationship with Anne the ways in which teachers can help and support each other through inquiry. I knew the benefits to be derived from trusting, collaborative relationships, and I continued to look for new ways to provide this situation for others, understanding this as improving my practice by emphasizing an "inside-out," as opposed to an "outside-in," approach to teacher development.

I collected data for my study in the form of field records and reflective material, collecting material on both the context of the study and on the study itself. I have described the kinds of data I collected and outlined my methods of collection in the next section.

The Collecting and Recording of Data

I collected data over a period of two and a half years and did so in two forms: that of field records and reflective writings. I kept field records and reflective material on both the context of the study and on the study itself, differentiating between these two kinds of data by keeping them separate. In order to do this, I set up various files within each of these sections, allocating different files to the different categories of data and storing it all on a microcomputer.

Field records consisted of descriptions of the inservice sessions, which were the context of the study, and field notes of the study itself, consisting of participant observation notes, journals, interviews, letters, interpretive accounts, and informal writings as a result of conversations, discussions, meetings, and planning sessions. Reflective writings were done in the form of journal writing and consisted of separate records of my observations of the context of the study and my observations of my collaborative work with Anne. Because Anne was a participant in my inservice and gave me her observations on the sessions, there was an overlap in this data, which I tried to keep separate by storing the data on our collaborative work together (whether inside or outside the inservice) separately from the other data on the context of the study.

The files containing the data on the context of the study contain detailed records of each workshop and reflective writings on the context of the study. The records contain material such as the proposed agenda for the workshop, the actual agenda experienced, the points raised for discussion, and the outcome of the discussions. The "minutes" of the workshop were written immediately after the session and were distributed to participants at the following session. In another file in this section, I kept an ongoing record of my own personal reflections, observations, and insights after each workshop and subsequent consultative sessions with any of the teachers in order to keep track of the issues raised and those needing to be raised in subsequent sessions. These records fulfilled two purposes—that of my study and that of a report to the board at the end of the year. The files containing the data on the study itself include anthropological-style field notes and reflective material. After each session with Anne, I made field notes on everything I had observed: student activities, observations of teaching, discussions with Anne, collaborative planning and teaching, the physical appearance of the classroom, and my own activities. My notes attempted to give a complete account of everything that went on and to record as much detail as possible. I was conscious of trying to enter into Anne's reality and to describe what I saw and heard, ruling out tendencies to interpret, judge, or synthesize while writing these field notes.

Once a week, I read over these transcripts, the records, and my own observations and recorded these reflections in a file entitled "Reflections on Reflections." These writings were my attempt to monitor my own learning and changing as a result of my experiences. I recorded my ongoing efforts to be a "facilitator of learning for teachers" as opposed to an "implementer" and my attempts to be the "responsive, reflexive and reciprocal" (Hunt, 1987) kind of consultant I wanted to be. I also wrote my own personal reflections describing the meanings of what I was observing, making tentative interpretations and wondering about the meaning of the teaching and learning that was going on for both of us. For the benefit of our growing understandings of each other, and in order to provide concrete accounts of our work together, I wrote many letters, interpretive accounts, and interview accounts that I addressed to Anne. We read them together, adding further insights and points of clarification, and I wrote them up as final collaborative accounts of aspects of our work together at that point in time. I have drawn all this material on the study itself together as field notes and have drawn on these field notes and on my reflective writings for all the stories I tell here. I have identified, wherever possible, the time when the field notes were written and thus the situation from which the details of a particular story or account are drawn.

CHAPTER 4

Image, Imagination, and Inquiry

A STRUCTURE FOR PROFESSIONAL GROWTH

> there is no end to that which,
> not understood, may yet be noted
> and hoarded in the imagination,
> in the yolk of one's being, so to speak,
> there to undergo its (quite animal) growth,
> dividing blindly,
> twitching, packed with will,
> searching in its own tissue
> for the structure
> in which it may wake.
>
> Thomas Kinsella, "Hen Woman," 1970

Anne's Image of Family Relations as a Meaning-Making Structure for Inquiry

I begin this chapter with a story of practice that shows Anne living out her life as a teacher within an understanding of her image of family relations and within an environment of interacting narratives. It shows the ways in which she understands herself as a teacher through responsive and responsible relationships with students and colleagues and through her experiences and interactions within those relationships. The details of the story expose the narrative threads that weave the text of Anne's life and show, too, the tensions that lie beneath the surface of that text. They highlight the ways in which Anne's own narrative is influenced by and is reconstructed through the process of struggling to reconcile felt tensions and to make new relations of the relations already at work in the environment.

The Nigglings

"This is a kid's life we're talking about," Anne said as she gathered together the papers she needed and prepared to leave the classroom. "I have a meeting with Rob [the principal] soon to see what can be done, so we won't be able to do any planning for the next day. I'll call you later this evening and we can talk about it then." I walked downstairs with her, and as we went, she explained that she was in a strange mood and worried about how it would all turn out. "I've had quite a bad weekend worrying myself to distraction about it all, as this kid has failed the year unless I can do something about it. I don't think this is right in this case, even though she has failed three subjects and that is the rule. Friday was the promotions day and lots of decisions were made, but this one thing has stuck in my mind all weekend, worrying me to distraction. You're not going to believe it, but because of all the anxiety over Cassandra, and wondering if I could find her some more marks, I rechecked all my marks this morning, and I found that I had miscalculated everything by 4%! Well, I adjusted them all, but it still was not enough to see her through, so I called Rob at lunch time and he is going to see me now."

It was a Monday afternoon at the beginning of June, and Anne had spent the weekend worrying about one of her students. The school policy for promotion to the next grade stipulated that a student should pass all subjects or attain a given average if there were failures, and Cassandra, with three failures, had not attained the overall average of 60% required. Anne explained that the situation had haunted her all weekend. "I was like a dog with a bone, looking at it in different ways, shaking it and turning it upside down and trying to make some sense of it. I even tried to talk myself into thinking that a failure might be a good thing for her and that she would benefit from another year in grade 8. That did not work because I know that she would be bored to death doing the same work again when she is capable of being in grade 9. All her friends will be in grade 9, too, and that will make matters worse because not only will she be disadvantaged by spending another year in the same grade but she will be humiliated by seeing her friends moving on. I think that maybe we made the wrong decision with regard to this kid, and there is a slight chance that it can be reversed, so I'm going to see what I can do. I'm going to tell Rob that I feel there's something not right here and that I don't think this kid should fail in spite of what the numbers say. I'll explain to him why I think that it would not be in her best interest to fail, and I know that he will listen and will support me even though he may not agree with me."

Two days later, Anne and I settled down in the team meeting room, tired after the school day but ready to talk about the lesson we had co-taught and how it had gone. I asked about the outcome of the meeting with Rob on Monday, and as I did so, Anne's face broke into a smile, and I knew what the outcome had been. "Well, now, there's an interest-ing story," she said. "It's almost like you know in your subconscious that there's something not right and that worrying about it and thinking about it will lead you to whatever it is. It was almost as if I knew that something was wrong, and it niggled me all weekend, ruining a lovely weekend at the cottage. I kept thinking of the kid and her life and how this would affect her, and I kept turning it over and over in my mind. I told Rob the whole story, the way I'd discovered the miscalculation in my marks because of it, everything, and he listened to the entire thing. I've said this before and now I'm going to say it again—that man is wonderful. Sometimes I don't believe it myself, but there aren't too many administrators who would listen and treat you the way he does. It is worth an awful lot to me to work with someone like this. At the end of it all he said, "It's what you think. We'll go along with what you think, you teach the kid and you know best. You know your students and I trust your judgment." Anne smiled at me and said, "Now who knows if I'm right or wrong, but I think I'm doing the right thing here, for this kid."

This story focuses on some of the narrative threads that link Anne's past, present, and future together and the way in which her life history is lived out in the classroom. The details of the story give insights into the way in which her narrative of family relations is acted out in her practice, the tensions that run beneath the surface of that practice, and the ways in which it is through the meaning-making structures of this image that she understands and lives within her world. I remember that the incident was filled with anxiety and tension for Anne as she told me about it on that Monday afternoon before she went to see Rob. The decision made regarding Cassandra was one that would negatively influence her future in Anne's opinion, and even though it had been made officially and according to just and rational premises, it was causing her anxiety. She was determined to oppose it on the basis of a different kind of justice.

As Anne told me the story before she went to see Rob, I had a sense of rehearsal and of her attempts to structure and to organize the ways in which she would present the situation to him through the telling. She spoke of doing "what is right for the kid," of the necessity for rules and for exceptions to the rules when "it is right for the kid." She also spoke of her confidence in being listened to and of being supported whatever the outcome. Thus it was that a situation that had started out as a problematic one resulted in a positive outcome for both student and teacher. It seemed to strengthen the bonds of Anne's relationship with Rob and to reaffirm to Anne herself the authenticity and integrity of her own story of herself as a teacher and of the unity of this incident within that narrative.

The Origins of Anne's Image of Family Relations

I want this place to be as much like home as possible so that students feel good and feel comfortable. It's just that I'm like that. Kids this age want *routines;* want someone to say "no," want someone to lay out the boundaries for them, but they also want that someone to be fair about it. I do think that students appreciate being treated as persons and that they grow in self-confidence and in self-worth as a result of being treated this way by me and by their peers. I really work at forgetting and starting afresh after a problem has been talked about and the kids seem to sense this. I can almost see and feel them wanting to get closer and to reestablish our relationship later on. They seem to go out of their way to make up for lost ground.

Anne wrote the words quoted here in the journal she kept for the first few months of our work together. She made approximately 10 entries in the journal; but because of the pressures of her workload and her commitments to people inside and outside her professional life, it became impossible for her to continue. We agreed that the writing she had done would become a part of my field notes but that the distinction between her written and spoken words would be acknowledged when quoted. The particular quotation is drawn from my field notes of February 1988 and it illustrates the interconnectedness of the personal and professional in Anne's life. It is in both her personal and professional lives that Anne's image of family relations originates, and Anne's relationships with family, friends, colleagues, and students are of primary importance in her life. Her sense of loyalty, commitment, and dedication to those with whom she is connected in these relationships is borne out in both her personal and professional decisions and actions, and it is within this context of family relations that Anne understands herself as a person and a teacher, reflects on her practices, and makes changes in her practice.

Anne experienced her teaching in the gym over the years as a member of several teams that team-taught, collaborated in the planning of programs, expected students to value one another's contributions and to work together. Anne told many stories of her days in the gym and of the various teams on which she worked. The following story, comprising sections from these stories, is told in order to evoke the meaning of Anne's understandings of herself as a teacher within the image of family relations.

Living and Learning as a Team

Carol and I worked together for eight years in the gym and we worked as part of a team. We supported each other and drew on each other's strengths, and that was very important for me. We did things together, constantly helped each other, talked about things and why they worked or did not work, and if one of us was not there, the other knew exactly what to do. We built up a lot of trust in each other and had a great deal of respect for each other, too. I love to have other teachers to work with, to share ideas with, and to learn with as we go along. This is how I learn best, and when I see or hear about things that might be an improvement on what I have, I figure out ways to fit them into my framework. I assess everything to see if it will make things better for the kids, and if I do not think that it will, I hold off and do what I think is important.

It is really important to have good team members (and I can say that because I've been on some good teams), and that was one of the best of them. Freddie was with us, too, and you can imagine how cut up we were at the break-up of the team when he died. It was from Freddie that I learned that I could smile and let a student know that I was disappointed, and that you get a lot more out of kids by cajoling, teasing, and jollying them along than by ordering them. When he was too ill to be at the school anymore, we used to bring him sandwiches from the delicatessen and try to cheer him up. We were a team, you see.

During my first year in the classroom, when I felt all alone and isolated, I drew on my colleagues in the staff-room for the support and help I needed. I remember hearing some of the teachers, after they had been to a conference, talking about ways of teaching students to work in small, cooperative groups in the classroom. The more I heard, the more I realized that I was hearing about ways to do in my own classroom what we had always done in the gym, and I became more and more interested in what I was hearing. Down there, we taught kids to work together, to depend on one another, to trust and respect one another, and to help one another along.

I tried out some of these ideas at the end of that first year, and I was very pleased with the results. It seemed to me that having the kids work together in partnerships and in small groups was the only way to settle them down and to feel that I was getting anywhere with them. The following May I went to the Cooperative Learning Conference and then did quite a bit of reading on cooperative strategies for the classroom during the summer. It all helped me to do what I wanted to do.

I believe that this story provides insights into the ways in which Anne stories herself as a teacher and in which she brings her professional and personal self, her values, and her beliefs to her current practice. It shows how the daily events of her life and her understanding of current situations are shaped and colored by her past experiences and by her image of family relations. It shows Anne's way of understanding teaching and learning as collaborative endeavours in which the lives of individuals are connected and in which the role of the teacher is one of creating and building relationships with students and among students and colleagues. It also shows the ways in which Anne's personal practical knowledge, shaped in past experiences, is brought forward to deal with the dilemmas of a new and problematic teaching situation.

The story shows, too, how Anne's understanding of herself as a teacher and her sense of self-worth are bound up with her ability to live out her image of family relations in the classroom and are inextricably linked to her ability to respond to and to be responsible to those with whom she is in relation, students and colleagues alike. Professional growth, "becoming a better teacher," and her efforts to develop professionally are understood in terms of the acquisition of the knowledge and abilities that allow her to respond to those with whom she is in relation and to teach and foster reciprocity within her relationships with students and among the students themselves.

Anne's way of knowing the world is supported by Gilligan's (1982) account of women's moral development, where she shows how women view themselves as living within a web of relationships and how important to them are caring and connectedness within all the relationships of which they are a part. "It is in their care and concern for others that women have both judged themselves and been judged" (p. 165). The effort to see people in their own terms is a characteristic that Gilligan ascribes to the women she studied, who demonstrated an ethic of responsibility as opposed to an ethic of rights. "The standard of moral judgment that informs [women's] assessment of self is a standard of relationship, an ethic of nurturance, responsibility, and care" (p. 165). This way of knowing emphasizes connection over separation, collaboration over competition, and understanding and acceptance over judgment and evaluation.

Anne's narrative of family relations provides the structures and the framework within which she understands and assesses her practice and determined the ways in which she gradually established, within her classroom each year, a community of learners who learned to work both independently and interdependently, who learned to relate to each other and developed the abilities to grow in their understanding of reciprocity, mutual understanding and autonomy as learners.

Image and Imagination Linked in Inquiry

Not in entire forgetfulness,
And not in utter nakedness,
But trailing clouds of glory do we come
From God who is our home.
Heaven lies about us in our infancy!
Shades of the prison-house begin to close
Upon the growing Boy...
....

At length the Man perceives it die away,
And fade into the light of common day.
                    (Wordsworth, "Ode: Intimations of Immortality")

As I began to write about Anne and to describe the details of her practices, I began to see the links between her image of family relations and the
way in which she made new relations and imagined new possibilities for
her practice. Unlike Wordsworth's Man, whose imagination faded and
died away as he got older, I saw that Anne's desire and abilities to make
new and different relations and more complex imaginative projections,
grew and developed through the process of inquiry. The link between
image and imagination, and the ways in which Anne's image of family relations provides the imaginative structures for her imaginative projections
can be seen and felt in the next story. This story was related to me by Anne
during one of our planning sessions, where it served then to direct our collaborative planning and decision making. The details took on a new level
of meaning for me at a later time, when I saw that they illuminated the
ways in which Anne constructed models for future practice and structured
the ways in which she projected her story into the future. Within the context of my exploration of the links between image and imagination, I saw
how the details of this story brought intellect and emotion together for
Anne, and the ways in which past experiences and the meanings she had
made of them structured the ways in which she made new relations, imagined new possibilities, and built a new world.

The Primacy of Experience

At the end of a school day in mid-November, Anne and I were sitting
in the team planning room next to Anne's classroom and waiting for the
last "good night, you two" in order to make some real progress with the
mythology unit we had started to plan. As our tentative ideas had
emerged, I had been recording them as a diagram, which was now begin-

ning to look like a huge spider's web. Anne looked at it, expressed her satisfaction with the way it was all turning out, and suggested that we add an oral presentation component to it, because of the benefits she believed students got from this. "It really helps them to understand and to value each other," she said. "At the end of last year, there was a situation where one of the weaker students was trying to express his ideas, and it was almost as if the others were reaching out to him, saying in body language, 'We know what you mean.' He was lost for vocabulary and when someone gave him the word, he was able to carry on, much to everyone's delight. I was really touched by this incident, and it happens every time I see students helping each other in this way. This is very different from the way it used to be, when their attitude toward each other's weaknesses was 'Ah-ha, we've caught you out.'" We agreed to schedule a few lessons to help students prepare for these presentations, during which they would have opportunities to practice expressing their ideas to small groups before doing so in front of the entire class.

This story shows how the story of Anne's professional development is inextricably linked to the classroom story she is living out and to the individual narratives of the students she teaches. Drawing on the personal practical knowledge of which her knowledge of adolescent students in general and of individual students in the class is a part, she determines the process and the content of the unit being planned, showing how she picks up the rhythms of students, gauges their knowing, adjusts, organizes, and plans according to their needs. Within this interaction of narratives—narratives of the students she teaches and others with whom she is in relation—Anne engages in a dialectical process where theory and practice support and confirm each other, and within which she continually structures and restructures her own narrative and ways of knowing.

Reflecting on the links between image and imagination through writing about Anne's practice, I began to probe my own understandings of the ways in which we know the world from our experiences, which then determines and directs the ways in which we think, decide, and act. I recalled the words of D. H. Lawrence, which had remained with me from the first time I had read them, and understood them in new ways within this context. Lawrence had said, "It is the way our sympathy flows and recoils that really determines our lives." Using them now, I began to make new connections and to understand their implications for teaching and within the lives of teachers. I found it possible to further explore the relationship between image and imagination, and to uncover the ways in which we build our future worlds and describe for ourselves the roles we will play in them, by focusing on the meaning of the experience of inquiry. Setting the stage for the exploration of the relationship between images grounded in experience and the imagination, which constructs possible models of human experience, required me to look again at image as a component of personal practical knowledge and, therefore, as a structural framework through which we think about the world in which we live and work and through which we construct new ways for thinking about it and living in it. Looking, then, at imagination, which Northrop Frye (1963) has defined as "a world of unborn or embryonic beliefs" (p. 31), "a place where the emotions and the intellect come together within the scheme of human affairs" and that has "the power of constructing possible models of human experience" (p. 5), I began to see that it is through image and imagination that we continually create and re-create the past, present, and possible futures of the worlds we live in.

The concept of image is used here in the way it was conceptualized by Clandinin (1986), as a kind of embodied knowledge that is a coalescence of diverse experiences from which new experiences are undertaken and that therefore provides a connection between an individual's past, present, and future. Image is also understood here within a theory of experience and of relations, as outlined by William James in the preface to *The Meaning of Truth* (1909), where he explains it thus:

> relations between things, conjunctive as well as disjunctive, are just as much matters of direct particular experience, neither more so nor less so than the things themselves....[and] the parts of experience hold together from next to next by relations that are themselves parts of experience. The directly apprehended universe needs, in short, no extraneous trans-empirical connective support, but possesses in its own right a concatenated or continuous structure. (pp. 6–7)

Things relating to and interacting with each other is what experience is, and it is how we relate to that experience that determines how we construct and reconstruct the meanings and understandings by which we live our lives. Pointing out that experience itself is "an achievement of aesthetic achievement...[and] an imaginative construction," Crites (1979) makes the link between image and imagination thus, "through imagination I develop the aesthetic forms within which my experience and my sense of personal identity take shape. That means that I form them, but they also form my conscious life" (p. 124). Through the process of reflection and inquiry, experience and imagination are linked in cyclical and rhythmic ways, where the imagination structures and colors experience and the way it is taken, which in turn determines future imaginings and future actions. The images we hold have been forged through our experiences and have emotional and moral dimensions, as did the experiences that shaped them.

Dewey (1934) describes emotion as "the moving and cementing force" in experience, as what provides "unity in and through the varied parts of experience" (p. 42); and morality, too, can be seen as grounded in experience, in that it is through our experiences that we develop our moral sensibilities. Thus the ongoing, daily flow of events, happenings, and routines come to us through our images, the constructs of which provide us with frameworks through which we reflect on them, give them meaning, and project their possible implications into the future—involving the learner intellectually, bodily, morally, and aesthetically in all acts of knowing and learning.

In *The Body in the Mind,* Johnson (1987) explores the ways in which meaning, imagination, and reasoning have their origins in our bodily experiences and develops a theory of how imagination links our cognitive and bodily understandings. He shows that it is through our "image-schematic structures" that we "construct our network of meanings and thereby direct and constrain our reasoning" (p. 139) and that "imagination is our capacity to organize mental representations (especially percepts, images and image schemata) into meaningful, coherent unities" (p. 140). He goes on to assert that "all meaningful experience and all understanding involves the activity of imagination which orders our representations (the reproductive function) and constitutes the temporal unity of our consciousness (the productive function)" (p. 157). He explains that the origins of our thoughts and the ways in which we think link our imagination to our experiences, an imagination that is "absolutely central to human rationality, that is to our rational capacity to find significant connections, to draw inferences and to solve problems" (p. 168). Our ideas, our imaginings, and our visions of the future, therefore, lie in our experiences, which shape the persons we are and the persons we can become.

Writing About the "Other-Than-I"

Anne's telling of her story of change as part of a presentation at the National Middle School Conference in Toronto, in October 1989, coincided with the beginnings of my struggle to find a way to tell that story in writing. I was entangled in a dilemma, which I understood as the impossibility of really telling the story of another's life, even though I had set out to do so. I could represent Anne faithfully as a character in my story, but could I write her story from her perspective and represent her faithfully as the central character in that story? Could I describe her world through her eyes and bring meaning to her feelings, her values, beliefs, and images of teaching and learning? I wondered and I worried.

The experience of hearing Anne's voice—confident, knowledgeable and assured—publicly outlining the significant aspects of her experience and describing our collaborative work from her perspective was significant for me. I heard of my role as a separate but valued subsidiary character in that story, one of the "others" with whom she was "in relation," and as the narrator of our collaborative experience. It helped me to search for the ways in which she frames her own stories of herself and in which she stories herself in her practices as I looked for a way to name the foundational structures of her understanding. I found that the terms *relationships, family,* and *team* emerged over and over again but was dissatisfied with each one in that some of the meanings associated with all of these terms were contradictory to my intended meaning.

Acknowledging that my difficulties were no different from those experienced by any responsible biographer, who, in writing another's life, must ensure that it is presented in the other's terms and understood through the other's images rather than those of the writer, I continued to explore. As I rejected one story and music metaphor after another, I became increasingly more conscious of the difficulty of getting hold of Anne's imaginative structures when my own structures continued to impose themselves on her world. Gradually, I came to understand and acknowledge the separate and interconnected components of the task, which required me to use my own imaginative structures to identify, to understand, and to write about those parallel structures by which Anne understands her life. I acknowledged my need to restructure my understanding of image within Anne's story as I had restructured it within my own, where I came to understand its embodied nature in new ways when I tried to write about it. I was reminded of a previous time in my life when, because of new experiences (which included the experience of "Jennifer and the Magic Butterfly," told in Chapter 1), I had begun to tell my story of teaching in new ways but did not retell the story within the context of my teaching as a department head until a later time. I could see the parallels in this new situation I was confronting.

To begin to understand Anne's embodied images, I returned to her stories and looked for the ways in which she herself imposes forms on her experience, and I heard again those accounts and descriptions of living and teaching within the context of relationships. Anne told stories of living as a child in a "community where people knew and cared about each other," of her family relationships, and of the people she had worked with over the years. In rereading those stories of family members, of people in the community, and of friends and professional colleagues, I found that for Anne the experience of being in a relationship had both joys and responsibilities. Then in exploring the various meanings of the terms *fami-*

ly, relationship, and *team* in both current and historical senses, I was surprised and delighted to find that *team* and *family* are related etymologically and that the contradictions I had perceived were due to current understandings but were not supported in a historical sense. (In the original Anglo-Saxon the word *team* means "family, set, animals harnessed in a row" and in modern English means "family, offspring" [Skeat, 1983, p. 544]). I decided that "family relations" conveyed the sense I believed Anne felt and that the meaning inherent in these words represented the ways in which she lived out her life. Over time, Anne continued to tell stories of being in supportive and supporting relationships, of friendships and working relationships, of teams, groups, families, and communities to which she has belonged and through which she has experienced the realities of her world and its "tempos, moods, patterns and projections" (Johnson, 1989, p. 372). As I began to see how her narrative of family relations describes the way in which she knows the world, I asked her how well she thought it described her classroom and herself as a teacher. Anne replied that she had never really thought of describing herself or her classroom in this kind of way, but that if she did, these words did describe her intentions and the way she feels about things.

I noted again how it was through stories that I had been able to work out my own understandings, to structure thoughts from the feelings I had about Anne's practices, and to imagine ways in which to articulate those thoughts through stories. In my attempts to interpret and understand the present by bringing it into a meaningful relationship with the past, I had reconfirmed again the power of my own image of story to structure my understandings and to create the imaginative frameworks that enabled me to extend them to understand others. In doing so I had restructured my understanding of image as I tried to understand it in the context of another's life and in the ways in which it structures feelings, understandings, reasoning, and methods of communication.

My purpose throughout has been to tell the story of professional growth and development and to choose those themes, facts, stories, and patterns that I have felt belong to that focus and that relate and contribute to the narrative unity of that story. However, I was constantly aware of what I perceived as the difficulties of telling another's story. As I collected, sorted, selected, and rejected from the multiplicity of stories that make up the fabric of Anne's life and are inextricably interconnected with one another, I became increasingly aware of the difficulty of the task in which I was engaged. As Barnes (1984) points out, the quality of the biography written is related to the skill and abilities of the biographer, and he likens the process of collection and selection to that of fishing with a net that he says can be defined as either "a meshed instrument designed to catch fish" or "a collection of holes tied together with string" (p. 38).

You can do the same with a biography. The trawling net fills, then the biographer hauls it in, sorts, throws back, stores, fillets and sells. Yet consider what he doesn't catch: there is always far more of that. The biography stands, fat and worthy-burgherish on the shelf, boastful and sedate: a shilling life will give you all the facts, a ten pound one all the hypotheses as well. But think of everything that got away, that fled with the last deathbed exhalation of the biographee. What chance would the craftiest biographer stand against the subject who saw him coming and decided to amuse himself? (p. 38)

The process of writing authentically about the "other-than-I" and the reconciliation of the differences between what has been experienced as "I" and as "other-than-I" caused me to become increasingly aware of the vibrancy and intensity of what I have experienced as "I," the bland and the exciting alike, compared to the flatness and the objectivity of that which has been experienced by the "other-than-I." I wrote many drafts in which I experimented with the possible relationships between form and content; drafts that ranged from displays of writing technique to objective pieces of reportage. None satisfied me in that they failed to show the qualities of the experiences they described or to portray the qualities of the persons of whom they spoke. The many drafts, my ongoing efforts to allow Anne's voice to be heard accurately and authentically and to describe the qualities inherent in her practice, brought me to new understandings of the process and was yet another circle in the spiral of a personal journey toward a greater understanding of myself as a writer and as a teacher. I have come to understand the difficulties and frustrations associated with the experience in terms of my struggle with control and creativity, with content and form, and with my ongoing relationship with writing. The experience, which was frustrating, fearful, and filled with uncertainty at the time, gave rise to a new series of beginnings for me, to the desire for increased understandings of the experience of the other and for greater writing capacities with which to express them.

CHAPTER 5

A Story of Change

LEARNING AND TEACHER DEVELOPMENT
THROUGH INQUIRY

Life itself consists of phases in which the organism falls out of step with the march of surrounding things and then recovers unison with it—either through effort or by some happy chance. And, in a growing life, the recovery is never mere return to a prior state, for it is enriched by the state of disparity and resistance through which it has successfully passed.... Here in germ are balance and harmony attained through rhythm. Equilibrium comes about not mechanically and inertly but out of, and because of, tension.... Form is arrived at whenever a stable, even though moving, equilibrium is reached.

John Dewey, *Art as Experience*

Making New Relations:
Constructing and Reconstructing Personal Practical Knowledge

After 29 years as a teacher, 26 of which were spent as a physical education teacher, Anne Courtney requested a change to a grade 8 core classroom. Anne made this change six years before retirement, taking on a situation that required her to teach most subjects at the grade 8 level, subjects that she had not taught before other than during a two-year period early in her career when she taught kindergarten for a year and grade 4 for another. The story of this major change in a teacher's life is treated here not as an isolated incident to be looked at by itself but set within the context of a life story within which it can be understood holistically and historically. It is the story of a time of loss and gain, of resistance and recovery, and of professional growth and development.

My story of Anne is biographical and temporal. It focuses on a time of her life when her transactions with her environment were problematic; the struggle to overcome the difficulties, the tensions, and the loss she felt in-

77

volved her in an inquiry within which intellect, emotions, and actions were focused on the construction of a new story of practice. Like the strings in a net that can be tied together in a pattern but that can also be untied and reassembled into other patterns, Anne's story is a temporal arrangement of the narrative threads of her life. In the light of a present that was not being experienced as expected or predicted, Anne's inquiry led her to re-arrange the narrative threads of her life into a new pattern and to tell a new and more significant story of herself, thus causing that lived past and expected future to become parts of a different whole. The growth and pro-fessional development that she experienced and the changed and restruc-tured story of herself she learned to tell were the fruits of this inquiry, and it is the story told in this chapter and in the one that follows.

The details of the construction of a new narrative are illuminated in this story of practice, which took place in Anne's third year in the core classroom and in the second year of our work together. At this time Anne had made significant changes to that practice and was rediscovering her enjoyment of teaching and feeling a renewed sense of professional com-petence and satisfaction. Anne had expanded the boundaries of the ways in which she knew her teaching, had come to know it in new ways, and was able to acknowledge the signs of her own creativity, adaptability, flexibili-ty, and growing acceptance of change. The story of her professional devel-opment is the story of her efforts to give voice to the story within her and to respond to the voices that flow in and continually influence the devel-oping narrative as she is living it out in her classroom.

> When they make the circle wide, it's time to swim
> out on your own and fill the element
> with signatures on your own frequency
> echo-soundings, searches, probes, allurements,
> elver-gleams in the dark of the whole sea.
>
> (Heaney, 1984, *Station Island*, p. 94)

An Introduction to Mythology: Introducing Other Voices

"My expectations are right up there now that I know what you peo-ple can do, so let's start by getting a few things straight and by listening. Stephan, how will I know that you are really listening to me now and to your group members once we begin? These books, posters, and materials you see around you are all for use during this mythology unit, and I have borrowed them from my husband. Treat them as you would treat anyone else's property, and don't mark them or put any sharp objects near them, or I'll never be able to wheedle his things away from him in the future. Aisha is in charge of things over there, and she will be keeping a watchful eye on things for me, won't you, Aisha? Robert, your log is in excellent shape, you've done a fine job here, and I can see that you are learning to be accountable for your work. This really helps me to know that you are keeping up with your classwork and with your homework. On Monday we are going to do a check on every one of you to make sure that you have all finished the first section, so be prepared for that. Those who have been slacking off have a busy weekend of homework ahead, and we all know better than to think we can get away with anything in this class. It's time to get busy now or the old lady will be on your case."

Anne's voice carried her words around a classroom that was as warm and colorful inside as it was cold and bleak outside, on this second day back in school in January. The white, snow-covered field outside the window and the ravine stretching out beyond it seemed to provide a silent and serene backdrop for the colors, textures, and shapes of the classroom and for Anne's voice, which was drawing the students' attention to the mythology unit they were about to begin and to the ways in which she wanted it to proceed. Anne walked around the room as she spoke, alternately sweeping the room with her eyes so that nobody would feel left out, focusing in on individual students, addressing them by their names, and commenting on their work. She moved effortlessly between the desks, using that teacher look that takes in the entire class with one sweep and monitoring what was behind her with the eyes that students all know experienced teachers like Anne have in the backs of their heads!

Anne was using her classroom voice, the one that she had learned in gyms and classrooms over the years and that projected itself around the classroom now, seemingly aware of those students seated farthest away from where she was standing and also of those students whose first language was not the one she spoke. Her clear tones simultaneously conveyed authority and compassion, commanding and caring. To a student in her class, her confident, assured classroom manner told of an experienced teacher—old enough to have seen and dealt with the usual tricks a student might think of to liven up the school day, and young enough to have the sense of humor to call herself an old lady, even though she looked no older than any of the parents when they got together on parent-interview night. To a parent or colleague, the story told by Anne's appearance—her short fair hair, lively blue-gray eyes, medium height and athletic build—would be one of a teacher in midcareer, and neither student nor parent would have guessed that this energetic, enthusiastic woman was even close to retirement. The least likely to guess would be those students who got up early in the morning and ran in the Kilometer Club she had organized before school a few mornings a week, several of whom were in this class!

As I entered the classroom, Anne was reminding the students of the class before Christmas when they had shared stories from their own cultures and of some of the stories they had told. She explained that the mythology unit would be a further opportunity to see how people from different cultures understood themselves and the worlds they lived in through their stories, myths, and legends. She went on to say that she had arranged with Ursula (the librarian) to show us an introductory filmstrip on mythology and to help us choose books and materials that we could keep in the classroom and use for the duration of the unit. We were to go to the library as soon as she finished speaking.

As I listened, my eyes swept the room, too, and I noticed how different things looked. The walls were covered with colorful new posters, pictures, charts, and maps; and filling the desks, which faced each other in groups of four, were 34 brightly clad adolescents, most of whom were proudly displaying the new sweatshirts and sweaters they had received as Christmas presents. The atmosphere was one of newness and new beginnings; a new year, new ways of working together, and a new unit about to begin. In the midst of it all, I noticed a few familiar things, too, such as the pots of geraniums ranged along the back window ledges, which now were bright with red blossoms, the "Countries of Origin" wallchart that remained on the wall, and the brightly decorated salutations in many languages that students had made as part of the Christmas celebrations. These were now interspersed between the new pictures of Greek and Roman gods and heroes, where they seemed to serve as a link between the students' own stories and the stories to come.

"I love this mythology unit," Anne had said to me the week before Christmas when the entire school, including Anne and her students, was buzzing with seasonal activity. She had shown me her tentative plans and said, "People around here think I'm crazy to be working on this every night and every spare moment during the day, with all the Christmas stuff going on, but I love it and that's my reason why. I've always wanted to do something on mythology, as I love it myself, and my husband does a unit on it every year with his students. I wouldn't try it by myself, but we can do it together because of your background, and that's one of the reasons why you are such a treasure to me. I want to be totally prepared for those first few weeks when we come back and when you look through these plans, you'll see that I've borrowed from everywhere, from all the other units we've done together, from the writing process, from cooperative learning, from English-as-a-second-language, and from everything that has been successful over the last few years. This is the cumulation of it all, and then I've added some new things, such as the letter to parents asking for their support and involvement both in the content and in supervising the homework aspect."

Settled down later in the library, Anne and I listened as Ursula asked the students what they knew about the origins and purposes of myths and legends. She asked them for examples from our own culture, and "The Terry Fox Story," "The Ben Johnson Story," and "The *Challenger* Disaster" were offered among many others. We watched the filmstrip that Anne and Ursula had chosen to give a brief historical backdrop to mythology, and then Ursula showed the students where they could locate the various kinds of books and learning materials they might want. As they searched through the card catalogs, shelves, and filing cabinets and began to load the book trucks with the fruits of their labors, we helped them until at one point Anne and I found ourselves close together; we stopped and stood and watched the entire scene being played out before us. We watched the students as they purposefully moved around the library, skimming encyclopedias and reference texts, carrying books to the tables, showing their findings to one another and helping one another out. "This is the highlight of my life right now," Anne said to me. "I really love to see the kids so involved, so obviously interested in what they are doing and helping each other too. This unit has some independent work in it, some group work, and some whole-class activities like today's. The kids are going to be reading, researching, sharing ideas and stories, collaborating with each other and with their parents, listening, viewing, and continuously assessing their own and each other's progress. These are all the things I want them to be doing, and I've got it all here. I want the unit to provide a bridge between the independence of the Olympics unit we did earlier and the interdependence of the novel unit that we will do later this year. I'm feeling really excited about getting into it, as I think that we will all enjoy it and get a lot out of it. It was on one of my trips to the cottage that I asked myself what I could do that would be really fun for the kids, fun for us to do together, and that would also integrate various aspects of the curriculum. The next step was that day when we started to plan and we bounced ideas off each other, the ideas all bubbling out and then down on the paper, one thing leading to another. I really felt the creative juices flowing then, and looking at what we have now makes me feel as if I'm really going somewhere."

Back in the classroom with all the new materials, Anne glanced at the clock, confirming that the period was nearly over, and congratulated the students for their purposeful and fruitful work in the library. She told them how at one point we had stood there together watching them and marveling at the industriousness of their researching and collecting. Then she said that she had been especially proud to see them helping each other and hoped that this would always continue. "I'm really excited about this unit," she said, "and Mrs. Beattie and I have had a lot of fun putting the plans together for you. I can see that you are enjoying it, too,

and I know that you will continue to draw on your parents for the stories, legends, and myths of your own people and your own cultures. In
the replies to the letter we sent out asking for their involvement and support, all the parents I heard from offered encouragement and all the help
we need. We are fortunate in this class to have so many cultures represented, and one glance at our wallchart shows us what a richness we
have here to share with each other."

Anne directed the students' eyes and attention toward the wallchart
"Countries of Origin," which was displayed beside the world map on
which the countries of origin of all the students had been highlighted. As
her voice read out the countries listed there—India, Rumania, Jamaica,
Tanzania, Guyana, Sri Lanka, Barbados, Ireland, Greece, Canada, Trini-
dad, St. Lucia, Zimbabwe, The Philippines, Scotland, Iran, Bulgaria,
Czechoslovakia—I thought of all the voices represented in this small
room, and I had a sense of the importance of what we were doing. I was
reminded of the day before Christmas when Togran had told his Persian
story in two languages and of the wonder we had felt at being introduced to a culture, a language, and a world beyond our individual experiences. Anne's voice was drowned out by the buzzer signaling the end of
the class and was then replaced by students' voices as they rose and left
the room, voices that gradually faded into the distance as they moved on
down the hall.

This story shows Anne in the process of making new relations from
the relations already existing in her environment and making "signatures
on [her own] frequency" (Heaney, 1984. p. 94). It shows how her image of
family relations provides the meaning-making structures within which
she understands herself and her practice and within which she gathers together the narrative threads of her past, projects them into the future, and
weaves a text for the present. It shows Anne in the process of combining
and varying the familiar components of her life to say something new that
will fit this particular classroom situation, adapting and improvising as
she does so and living out her values, beliefs, and passions in her practice.
It shows Anne in the process of creating a curriculum for her classroom, a
process in which the personal and the professional are linked in inextricable ways and which is creative, adaptive, rational, logical, emotional, and
value-laden.

The story highlights the ways in which Anne understands her practice,
the improvement of her practice, and her own professional development
through increased responsiveness to the voices of those with whom she is
in relation, within the community to which she belongs. Noddings (1986)
has described this way of knowing and being as "fidelity to persons," and

viewed from the perspective of an ethic of caring, it has the quality of relations at its heart. Within this way of knowing, self-actualization and personal development revolve around the acquisition and refinement of skills and knowledge that will build increased relational competence and the ability to empower others with whom one is in relation through the attainment of "high fidelity." Guided by her image of family relations, Anne is shown making choices among curriculum content and teaching strategies and is seen choosing those that will benefit students as persons, will expose them to the richness and diversity of their own voices and to the voices of others, and will promote and teach understanding, appreciating, valuing, and cooperating among them. Anne provides classroom experiences through which students are taught how to listen, how to respond and to relate to one another so that they can enter each other's understandings, allow the narratives of others to interact with their own, and allow other voices to flow in and to influence their own developing voices.

In striving for "high fidelity" (Noddings, 1986), Anne structures the inquiry through which she makes new relations between aspects of the narrative of her life and describes a new role for herself as a teacher and new roles for students, for subject matter, and for the classroom as a place for learning. Through listening and responding to the sounds of her own changing voice and to those voices which speak of essential and authentic aspects of herself and her experience—the voices of students, parents, colleagues, administrators, policy makers, and those who belong to her immediate and larger social, political, and cultural milieu—these narratives become connected to her developing narrative and to the narrative of the classroom. In the living out of her changed story and in those places where her narrative can be seen to interact with those of others, such as in her collaboration with Ursula, with Robbie, with Kate, and with me, students can see and hear the tones, the patterns, the rhythms, and the cadences of collegiality, collaboration, fidelity and family relations.

Interacting Narratives:
The Hallowed Ground Where Lives Meet Lives

The most prevalent problem I had [in the first year] and still have with each new class lies in the way that many students see the classroom as a competitive rather than a collaborative place. I find that I have to spend time and energy helping them to develop the social and communication skills whereby they can work together and gain an appreciation for the strengths and talents of others. When they've worked in groups for a while, I notice a real change in their attitude toward each other. They become more understanding of each other, more willing to help each other, more supportive and encouraging, and this is really important for them.

Anne wrote the words quoted above, and I have drawn from my field notes of March 1987. Anne's words help to explain her interest in small-group learning, in cooperative learning, and in teaching students to collaborate with one another. The context within which she began the mythology unit was one of the multiple organizational, program, and personnel changes associated with the official change to middle school. Teachers were grouped together in grade teams to provide multidisciplinary programs to heterogeneous classes of grades 6, 7, and 8 students, and the school day now included a daily advisory class to be taught by the core classroom teacher and many extracurricular activities. Anne's core grade 8 class was comprised of two distinct groups: the English-as-a-second-language (ESL) students, who were indeed very diverse but whom Anne had become accustomed to teaching, and a very wide-ranging group of regular grade 8 students. Anne had been feeling increasingly more competent in teaching the ESL students; but she was now concerned about having so much diversity in the same class at the same time as she taught a number of new subjects and tripled the number of students to whom she related in a four-day cycle.

The experience of the change to the middle school was not as Anne had expected, even though she had planned ahead in order to be ready and felt that she had learned a lot from her experiences of the previous two years. In this, her third year in the core classroom, when she had expected to be "in control," Anne was experiencing a new change situation because she was now teaching 250 students in a four-day cycle, teaching a number of new subjects, and dealing with a new organizational structure. She was now responsible for teaching English, history, geography, advisory, computers, math, and science to her own core grade 8 class, physical education to four combined grade 8 classes, and guidance to four grade 6 classes. By November of that year, she was feeling very frustrated about her teaching. She was dealing with a wide range of subject matter that she did not feel she knew well enough to be teaching it. She was also teaching such a large number of students that she felt she could not get to know them as individuals and therefore could not be a good teacher.

Anne found the pressure of trying to respond to so many voices to be overwhelming and dispiriting, and the mythology unit was her attempt to deal with the many voices she was hearing and to incorporate the narratives of others into the narrative of the classroom. Prior to the beginning of the unit, Anne wrote a letter to parents to tell them of its purpose, its planned length, and the work expected from students, some of which would of necessity be done at home. She had asked parents for their support and encouragement in the collection of stories and in the monitoring of students' work. Anne began the mythology unit by having students talk to their parents about the customs and celebrations of their different cultures and then telling these stories to one another as part of the Christmas celebrations in the classroom. Her letter had invited parents' voices into the classroom arena and had endeavoured to push the boundaries of the classroom narrative out to include their voices, their concerns, and their stories. Anne felt the tension between narratives acutely; it was a tension which drove her inquiry, which directed the ways in which she dealt with it, and out of which grew the professional development she desired for herself. This next piece, taken from my field notes of January 1988, illustrates the ways in which Anne felt those tensions and engaged in a struggle to reconcile them within the structures of her image of family relations.

The Tensions Between Narratives

I'm feeling pressure from all sides, from parents who asked at interview night, "Is the class behind because of the English-as-a-second-language component and the behavior problems we hear about?" "Why don't these kids get more homework? They never seem to do any at home." I feel it from higher administration when there's all this talk about effective schools, and if they bring back standardized testing as they are talking about doing and assessing these kids' progress in ways that can be measured, all my efforts are in vain...It comes from the media daily, too, and they seem to be criticizing education at every opportunity...In the middle of all this, I'm on a rollercoaster trying to keep up with the content in all these subject areas to the extent that if I take a Saturday morning off, I feel guilty...I'm tired of living in the small world of "I" in order to survive...out of control and tired of not being able to live up to my responsibilities in my relationships outside school. This unit on mythology is helping me to get this one corner of my life under control...It is giving me somewhere to go...I know that I'm doing all that is possible within the circumstances and that when I'm so focused on survival it is virtually impossible to think of anything else.

As I explored Anne's stories I began to hear the patterns of listening and responding to her own voice and to the voices of others, as well as the tensions associated with her inability to respond in the ways she wanted to. I began to see the frameworks through which she understood and directed her inquiry and made increasing sense and meaning of her situation of change as she negotiated between the competing demands on her attention, her time, and her energy within the interacting narratives of her life. By focusing her inquiry into one area of her teaching at a time, such as the mythology unit, she worked on "getting one corner under control" and on using the tensions she felt to construct and to establish a coherence within her own narrative through which she could then become increasingly more responsive and reciprocal to the voices of others. From this one secure and stable vantage point, she then extended her practices into other areas of her teaching and toward the creation of more new forms where multiple voices could be heard within an increasingly harmonious and balanced unity.

Anne often used the word *play* to describe the work we did together in the classroom and the kind of approach we used as we planned and taught together, as we did in the mythology unit. For Anne, *playing* meant trying out new strategies and ideas, observing closely how students responded, discussing the advantages and disadvantages of a given approach, considering other possibilities for how it might have been done, and sometimes extending these practices to other areas of the curriculum. It was mainly during the planning sessions that she articulated the possibilities she was imagining and thereby provided me with insights into that process that she called *play*. I was coming to understand Anne's notion of play as the process of allowing herself to imagine other than she knew, and of trying things she had not already worked out rather than doing as she was used to doing in the past, within the structures and frameworks of a collegial partnership. I understood our collaboration as playing together in a musical sense and used to describe what we were doing as improvising on the theme we had selected, combining and adapting what we each knew to co-create something to fit the unique and particular situation we were in. We listened and described variations on each other's melodies, we played together and in unison, and we experienced the aesthetic satisfactions of the emerging forms we were co-creating. Like Clandinin (1993) and her colleagues who tell collaborative stories of teacher education, we had only "the sketchiest of plot outlines to follow as we began our inquiry," and we, too, were engaged in "what Bateson (1989) would call a desperate improvisation, for we were engaging in what we knew would be an inquiry in which there were many ways of knowing, many ways of making sense and many institutional stories" (Clandinin, 1993, p. 8).

I have come to understand the collaborative process that Anne and I experienced in terms of the very difficult process by which we were each trying to bring the retelling and the reliving of our stories into closer harmony. Individually, we were each trying to make greater coherence of the conflicting elements of our lives and using the tensions we felt to drive and direct us through the circling, spiraling, storytelling journeys in which we were engaged. Through our collaboration, our individual narratives interacted and influenced each other as we improvised and co-created a curriculum for the classroom. I would describe our work together as a joyful improvisation. I have beautiful memories of many of the experiences we had and of the feelings and satisfactions we shared as we acknowledged our delight with some of the things we were making together.

As Anne described a new role for herself as a teacher who created forms of practice that would give students opportunities to enter into the understandings of others and to come to new understandings of themselves, she did so through the creation of spaces where narratives were allowed to interact, to flow in and influence each other. The following story of practice is about one of those times in classroom life where such a space and a setting are created for narratives to interact and for lives to touch lives. The story is about one of those times when something magical happens, a time when the atmosphere of openness, acceptance, and confirmation allows understandings to flow in and to influence the hearer, a time when, in John Donne's word, spirits "interanimate" each other. It describes an environment within which the world of the other can be glimpsed and more than the self imagined and within which shared systems of understanding and communication can be created. The effect of such incidents on the lives of some of those present is powerful, immeasurable, unforgettable, and potentially transforming. I have drawn from my field notes of December 1988 to construct this story of Anne's classroom practice.

Togran's Story

Togran told the Persian folk tale about the king who had three sons to the group of students who gathered around him and listened as if their lives depended upon the outcome. When he finished, Laura asked, "What does Persian sound like? Can you say something in Persian?" Togran spoke a few sentences in an exotic-sounding language to listeners whose delight was written all over their faces, and then Ingrid said, "What about the writing? I wonder what Persian writing looks like? Can you write anything?" Reaching for some chalk, Togran turned and wrote four vertical symbols that he told us said "How are you?" in Persian, and then he sounded them out. We each did our best to replicate what he had said, rolling the sounds around in our mouths, looking at each other for help, and then breaking down and laughing at how ridiculous we sounded, all talking at once and without an intelligible sound coming from any of us. Looking over at Laura, Togran said, "I could tell the whole story in Persian if you liked." The admiration and wonder on the faces of the group members was plain to see as Laura turned to me and said, "I think the whole class should hear this." Anne was working with the other half of the class, but we gathered them all together as Togran made his way to the front of the room and proceeded to write the name of the story in Persian symbols and in English on the front blackboard. Then he sat down on the high stool and waited for us to settle. He looked so pleased, so comfortable and at ease, and so obviously proud of his heritage and of his ability to speak its language and to tell its stories.

It was the week before Christmas, and the entire school was alive with activity and excitement as students and teachers were busily engaged in preparations for the carol singing, the school concert, contests for best classroom decoration and best door decoration, and the long-awaited and, in every case, well-planned upcoming classroom party. My walk down the hallway had been a visual feast, as the "Best Door Decoration Contest" had brought out the creative talents of numerous students; and looking through these colorful and heavily disguised classroom doors, I had seen classrooms bedecked with streamers and decorations of many kinds. On reaching Anne's classroom I saw that it, too, had been transformed into a magical place where student-made decorations and artwork were hanging from the ceiling and displayed on every wall, filling the room with a richness and variety of colors, shapes, and textures. Anne's students were celebrating the season by sharing stories of incidents, events, and customs from their countries. Having interviewed their parents to get a selection, they had each chosen one story to tell to a small group of colleagues. The activity was also an introduction to the mythology unit that Anne was preparing for when they came back after Christmas.

It was within this setting that Togran prepared to tell his story, which he did first in English and to which the audience listened without a sound. Starting then at the beginning of the story, he told it again line by line, first in Persian then in the English translation. We were spellbound, 35 students and Anne and myself, all experiencing an atmosphere that was nothing less than magical. The sounds of the unintelligible but musical Persian language rolled off Togran's tongue, only to be followed by the familiar sounds of English giving us the next part of the storyline and requiring from Togran the invisible but nonetheless amazing mental gymnastics of moving from one language into the other and back again. When he paused, we seemed to hold our collective breath and to breathe out again when he picked up the threads and wove the patterns of the story right in front of us. He smiled as he finished, and the class broke out into a storm of clapping that spoke of communal pride, of appreciation, of valuing, and of absolute admiration. He made his way back to his desk, where he sat down, smiling and openly enjoying the response he was getting.

The Experience of Change:
Losing Voice and the Struggle to Regain It

> And who ever heard
> Such a sight unsung
> As a severed head
> With a grafted tongue.
>
> Old Celtic rhyme

Anne's decision to change to the core classroom six years before retirement was made "for many reasons, the most important one being that I felt I needed a change. I was very comfortable in my situation, and things were going very nicely, but the edge was gone and I just wasn't having any fun any more. I wanted to get that edge back." (Courtney, Conference Presentation, October 26, 1989.) Aware also of the upcoming official change to middle school in two years time and wanting to plan ahead and to deal with the change in her own way, Anne requested the change as "an opportunity for professional challenge and growth" and was surprised and disappointed to find that the experience of the change was not as she had expected or imagined it to be. She felt pain, anxiety, and frustration before she felt the rewards and benefits she had expected and looked forward to.

In 1987, when I met her and she was in the second year of the change, in addition to her classroom teaching, Anne was involved in several school-based professional activities, one of which was the school's Middle School Implementation Committee, where she worked to organize and design the framework and structures of the future middle school. Throughout her career, Anne had always been involved in a wide range of school and board committees and extracurricular activities ranging through organizing and supervising outdoor education excursions for students, serving as an associate teacher for student teachers, writing curriculum documents for teachers, and teaching adult education courses in health and fitness. She also took courses in subjects that interested her, and her personal interests range through subjects as diverse as music, baseball, astronomy, geology, and bird-watching. In her learning experiences inside and outside school situations, Anne expected them to be social, purposeful, enjoyable, and a balance of "learning, thinking, maximum participation, and fun."

In her second year in the classroom, Anne initiated a program which would bring Robbie, the ESL teacher, and Kate, the special needs resource teacher, into her classroom to work directly with students instead of with-drawing them, as had been the case prior to this. The results of this pilot program became the basis for the integration of ESL students throughout the school and for the collaboration of ESL, special needs, and core class-room teachers. "Aren't teachers supposed to be burned out at this stage of their careers?" I had once asked her as I questioned her energy and enthu-siasm for new ventures and for change and challenge. She had replied, "We've talked about this at home, too, as we are both just a few years away from retirement. Our motto is that we live for what is happening now and make the most of it. Who ever knows what's coming?"

Anne had entered the situation of change with enthusiasm and inter-est, and in her first year in the core classroom she did not expect the ex-periences that came and the feelings she had toward them. In describing how things fell apart in her teaching life, Anne re-creates the experience retrospectively, her words echoing those of Yeats

> Turning and turning in the widening gyre
> The falcon cannot hear the falconer;
> Things fall apart; the centre cannot hold.
> Mere anarchy is loosed upon the world,
> The blood-dimmed tide is loosed, and everywhere
> The ceremony of innocence is drowned…
>
> (Yeats, "The Second Coming," p. 211)

Anne's story is told here to describe the experience of change as she ex-perienced it during that first year in the core classroom. The details of the experience came out in a series of conversations, which I had recorded in my field notes as Anne told them to me over time. My efforts to represent the experience through story were greatly assisted by Anne, who verified and authenticated the content, the tone, and the sequencing of the details of this story, as she did with all the others also.

The First Year in the Core Classroom

My first year in the core classroom was a very uncomfortable, lonely, and frustrating time during which I rarely felt competent or confident about what I was doing. The picture I have of myself at this time is of me standing in the mire up to my chin, just barely moving in any direction, floundering around and asking questions of all and sundry. I felt out of

control, disorganized, and incompetent most of the time, never feeling
that I was good enough; and this I believe accounted for my constant
feelings of guilt and frustration.

In the gym, I used to think of myself as a solid teacher, very practical
and knowledgeable in my subject area, and I also considered myself to
be well organized, competent, and confident. During that first year, I felt
like a beginning teacher again, overwhelmed, anxious, and unsure of
everything, and flooded with hundreds of questions that needed to be
answered at any given time. Every day meant finding out how little I knew
about something or other, and I spent my evenings trying to keep ahead
and searching out the information I needed, always two centimeters
ahead of the kids and doing the best I could. I did not feel that I had the
necessary knowledge or skills to do the kind of job I wanted to do, and I
felt isolated and lonely after the team-teaching situation I was used to in
the gym.

I remember those first months as really frightening, and looking back
now, I recognize that the intense anxiety I felt during the entire first year
was chiefly associated with the pressure I felt to give the students a good
program and feeling my inability to do so. I cared about the kids and
about the program they were getting, and I acknowledged the complexity
of the situation. We had at least 15 different cultures and nationalities
represented in that class, and the language abilities ranged from those
who spoke no English at all to those for whom it was the mother tongue.
I felt unable to meet the needs of such a wide-ranging group, and when I
thought about how my students were missing out because of my inadequacies, those feelings really hurt. My self-confidence, self-esteem, and
sense of self-worth were dealt one blow after another until I wondered
how much I could actually stand. I had expected some difficulties, but I
had not anticipated anything like this. I often heard that this was supposed to be a "growth time," but I certainly was not experiencing any of
the joys of growth!

Those who helped me most were the ones who answered my multi-
tudinous and ongoing questions and who gave me the feeling that it was
all right to ask and to keep on asking. I had decided that this was the
only way to go...when in doubt, ASK; and I *knew* deep down that I would
work things out one way or another. I also knew that there really was no
easy way of solving the issues and that there were no superficial or expe-
dient answers to my problems. I remember thinking how ridiculous it was
to be feeling this way, when I had so many years of experience, but I did-
n't know where to start. At the height of my insecurities, I knew that I
could call on central consultants for help, but at that time I didn't feel
secure enough to invite people into the classroom to help me until I had

things under control and my kids were treating one another like human beings. When this was in place, I could deal with the guidelines and other people's expectations and I could avail of that outside support.

My husband was my main source of support, and he was the one who helped me to realize that my focus had to be on getting some kind of control within the room, giving me numerous suggestions of ways in which to establish a classroom environment in which students would respect and listen to each other. He also helped me with the content of the courses and with the lesson plans I was preparing every night at home. My friends helped me, too, and reinforced my feeling that curriculum content could not be the top priority until I had established an environment in which students showed some respect for one another and for me. I made it my first priority to teach them the social skills they needed to achieve this, as these kids thought nothing of shouting out whenever they had something to say, hiding under desks, editorializing on every comment I made, chewing gum, and being rude to one another. It was March of that first year before I felt that I could claim to have achieved any success.

My frustrations had physical effects, too, as I spent the night clenching my teeth; in the morning I'd wake up with very sore jaws. That year, it was the long weekend in August before the knots were out of my stomach and I could eat a meal without indigestion afterward. My feet hurt, too, because I wore regular shoes consistently for the first time in many years instead of runners. I could hardly believe that the change would have such an effect on me, but there was nobody to blame but myself, as I knew that I needed a change and a challenge. These totally unwelcome and somewhat surprising side effects as part of the situation had not been anticipated, but as time went on, things began to come together for me. Gradually I began to feel that I was gaining control, not just of what was going on in the classroom, but also of the new subject matter and the ways of teaching it.

During this time I wondered if all this may have had just a little bit to do with age and number of years teaching, as I have heard others of my vintage talk about being in similar situations. I wondered whether I had become so set in my ways that I was too easily thrown off balance and inflicted with "hardening of the lines of flexibility." Later on, when we did make the official change to middle school and I heard all my colleagues tell of feeling the stresses of change as I had felt them, it always made me feel a little better knowing that I was not alone. When we talked and shared advice then, it did us all good, knowing that we all had the same feelings and were feeling the same inadequacies, but during that first year, I had experienced them alone.

I tell this story of Anne's experience of her first year in the core class-room because she articulates so vividly what the experience of change feels like when the story being lived is not as it had been expected or imagined. Her story describes what it actually feels like to be "out of step with the march of surrounding things" (Dewey, 1934, p. 14) and to be conscious of the "split between [her] present living and [her] past and future" (p. 18). The story she held, with its interconnected past, present, and future, did not fit the situation she was experiencing, and the split between the telling and the living of her story was one that caused her to feel anxiety and pain and to be physically and emotionally exhausted instead of energized and renewed. It also caused her to experience feelings of "not seeming to be get-ting anywhere," instead of the feelings of professional development and growth that she had expected, imagined, and looked forward to.

Anne described the experience of living in the split between the told story and the reliving of that story as "feeling like a first year teacher" and "not even knowing where to start." She explained that she felt she had to deal with more information and external expectations than she could re-alistically handle. She felt the frustrations, the confusion, the complexi-ties, the seeming hopelessness, and the profound mystery of trying to do what was good for each of her students when she did not know what this was, how she could determine what it was, or how to achieve it even if she knew what it was. She was trying to deal with all that at the same time as she responded to the needs and requests of those others with whom she was in relation and who also had an interest in what went on in her class-room. It was out of a deep empathy with Anne and her difficult situation that I wrote the following poem. Anne's reaction to it was of surprise and delight that I had managed to represent her felt experience so completely.

> Would you believe me
> If I admitted that what I really felt
> Was the dispiriting, disappointing,
> flat dullness of seeming to be getting nowhere?
>
> If I described the constant feelings of guilt
> Of inadequacy and of shame,
> And if I spoke of shrivelling and shrinking
> Instead of changing and growing,
> Would you understand?
> Would you?
>
> (Beattie, "Change," September 1990)

Anne had experienced what Schön (1987) described as the paradox of learning a really new competence and the discomfort associated with it.

Schön points out that "a student cannot at first understand what he needs to learn, can learn it only by educating himself, and can educate himself only by beginning to do what he does not yet understand" (p. 93). Yet by the end of her first year in the classroom, Anne was dealing with this paradox through relationships; drawing on the relationships in which she was involved for help and support and in order to begin to establish relationships among her students in the classroom. Anne explained how she had dealt with her situation in a presentation about how she had established small-group learning situations in her classroom that she made to her colleagues as part of the inservice program in which we were all engaged. She agreed to do this in order to help other teachers who were struggling with the same issues with which she had struggled. As Anne heard the echoes of her own story reflected back to her colleagues, these echoes informed and influenced the new story she was trying to live out. In this next piece, I have drawn from the field notes I took during Anne's presentation in May 1989, and in the writing of the story, I received additional information and details from Anne. As in the case of all the stories I have written in Anne's voice, this story was authenticated by Anne as representing, in a written form, the meanings she intended to express in her spoken words.

Learning to Work Together and Learning About Relationships

All students need to be able to work with others, and I believe that it benefits them academically and socially when they learn how to do so. I notice a real change in their attitude toward each other after they have worked together for a while. They become more understanding of each other, more willing to help each other, more supportive and encouraging, and this is really important for the students I teach.

I began by building routines and structures and by insisting that the students show respect for me and for one another. Then we established what was acceptable behavior so that the classroom would be a good place for everybody. Shouting out, being rude, and all kinds of disruptive behavior were not allowed, and when inappropriate behavior occurred, as it inevitably did, everything was brought to a halt and there was instant retribution to make. This usually took the form of 10 push-ups or sit-ups, to be done immediately, or else returning at the end of the day to stay with me instead of going to Home Unit. This is Anne, the physical education teacher, asking for immediate payment, as I disliked having kids come back five hours later for after-school detentions. I could see and feel their anger sometimes, but I held to the routines we had agreed to. I knew also that my expectations for their behavior were not easy for some of them, but I also think that they appreciated being treated as persons. I believe that kids grow in self-confidence and in self-worth as a result of being treated this way by me and by their peers. I really worked then, and always do, at forgetting and starting afresh after a problem has been talked about, and I don't hold any grudges or carry over any bad feelings. The kids seemed to sense this, and I could see and feel them wanting to get closer and to reestablish our relationship later on. They seemed to go out of their way to work harder and to be more friendly toward me to make up any lost ground. I have always believed that kids this age want routines, want someone to say "no," want someone to lay out the boundaries for them, but they also want fairness in everything, and this group reinforced my belief.

When I introduced some group work toward the end of my first year in the core classroom, the kids loved it, and it really helped me to begin to get things under control, as it seemed to be the only thing that got them involved in the work. I heard about cooperative learning in the staff-room from Ben and a few others who had gone to a conference. The more I heard about it, the more I realized that here were some strategies to help me to do in the classroom what we had always done in the gym. I went to the conference myself the following year and then went through these cooperative learning books from cover to cover in the summer. I picked out several strategies that I could use to help my students to develop the social skills they needed, to learn to respect one another and work together and help one another to learn the subject content. Then I made plans to start as early in the year as possible.

I always begin now with partnerships and by encouraging students to help one another to do something that they are doing individually. At the beginning of the year they look at me as if to say "Are you crazy?... Help each other?... Why would we do that?" Gradually they get used to the idea that if you can do something and your partner cannot, you should help him or her. I continue to emphasize the importance of working together, of helping one another and of acknowledging and recognizing one another's abilities and strengths. I make sure that they have plenty of opportunities to practice listening to one another, focusing on really hearing what the other is saying and building on what is said, acquiring a vocabulary for giving nonjudgmental feedback, and getting comfortable with giving and receiving feedback. I structure situations where they have to listen to one another carefully, to help one another to clarify or to extend their ideas, to take turns in talking, and to have concern for the questions, concerns, and needs of the other within the partnership. When I feel that they are ready, I then set up situations where two sets of partners join together to make a group of four, and they can be given a larger project to work on. Now they have to take responsibility for, and to be accountable for, a part of a larger piece of work, to be concerned about three other people, and to begin to learn the complex dynamics of working with three others in this larger-group situation.

I start by explaining to students that the answers to their ongoing questions are to be dealt with within the group and explain that before asking me for help, they are first to ask a partner or group member for the answer or for help in locating the information in the resource books. Gradually they begin to see one another as resources, to begin to learn from one another, to develop their self-confidence and self-esteem by helping others, and to learn the social skills necessary for working with others.

Anne understood her situation of change as a multifaceted one within which her first priority was to "establish control in the classroom," and to get things to "fall into place" in the way they were in place when she taught in the gym. As a "competent, confident, and secure" teacher who was proud of her sense of professional worth, Anne was angered and pained by her inabilities to live out the expectations she held for herself in the new classroom environment, and while she struggled with these feelings and perceived inabilities, the students she taught were not treating her or one another in ways that she considered acceptable. Anne felt a need to deal with all these issues simultaneously and immediately. She also felt that she needed to acquire new knowledge in the subject areas in which she was teaching, to deal with the details and directions of ministry and board guidelines in each of these subject areas, to master new and recommended teaching and evaluation strategies, and to acquire the knowledge and skills with which to put all this together in different situations of practice and with different groups of students.

It is strangely ironic that as Anne began to identify and to hear the sounds of her own voice resounding from her practice, and to begin to make a coherent message of what she heard, her life was filled with too many voices, all raised together to provide policies, implementation strategies, directions, priorities, and thrusts. Raised together they had the effect of drowning out the tentative and developing sounds of her own voice and rendering her voiceless and powerless at a time when her personal voice and personal power were critical for professional growth and development. The effect created by too many voices, all presenting competing parts of a narrative for the classroom, created an uneducative experience for Anne, which was in complete contrast to the positive, educative, growth-oriented experience she had anticipated. The following story, the details of which were drawn from the field notes written during the span of the research period, gives insights into the meaning of this experience for Anne and into both the potentially constructive and destructive qualities of a situation of change.

A Cacophony of Competing Voices

During those first two years, when I was trying to get myself organized, going to meetings was a real challenge for me. I found them very dispiriting and frustrating, and I would come away from some of them feeling totally overwhelmed and wiped out, seeing too many things coming in on me and feeling swamped. It seemed to me that I would be just about getting things in order in my classroom when I would be confronted on many sides by all the different guidelines I should be implementing and the different kinds of teaching strategies I should be using. There never seemed be any time to figure anything out before the onset of another series of pressures and external expectations. Colleagues such as Harry [the department head] helped me every way they could, and I knew that he understood that I was doing my best. However, I could also hear the voice of that parent asking me whether her daughter was not being held back because she was in this class, and I could see in front of my mind's eye those guidelines and the curriculum content that I was not getting to, and I would feel awful. The expectations seemed endless, as did the difficulties of living up to everybody's expectations, each new wave of which brought feelings of being out of control and filled me with self-doubt, worry, and anxiety all over again.

I remember feeling a real sense of panic at one of these meetings when we were given a list of things we were supposed to be doing in that one subject area alone (writing folders, status of the class, writing process, group work, individual novels...), then given a checklist and told to tick off those we were doing. I was not doing half of the things on the list and could not see any way that I could be, given the diversity of the students I was teaching and their unfamiliarity with working in these new and different ways. I allowed myself to panic a little and then to work things through in my own way, so that they were somewhat more realistic, knowing that I had to concentrate on sorting out the situation in the classroom and then deal with policies, guidelines, and the concerns of others in my own ways.

My whole tone of voice changes when I am confident about my subject. But you ask me about English and I have this small, insignificant, squeaky voice. When I'm talking about anything to do with physical education, it is an entirely different matter, because I know something about that and I talk about it in a confident way that shows how I feel about it. I think everyone can hear that in my voice.

Anne's story describes the anxiety, the pain, and the stress caused by her inability to find the space and the silence within which to deal with the tensions she was feeling, to hear her own voice, and to use it to construct the tentative structures, the rhythms, and the plot of a viable story for her situation. Until she could bring a coherence and a unity to the narrative that formed the central unity of her own life, Anne could not make coherent meanings of the isolated parts of different conceptions of a narrative for the classroom being offered by other voices, and she could not assess, understand, or incorporate them into her own narrative. As she struggled to live out the future of a told story that was playing itself out in unexpected ways and no longer appropriate to her situation, Anne found it necessary to tell and to retell that story in her search for coherence, harmony, and unity in her life.

I have come to understand Anne's experience of change as the experience of living with the tensions between the retelling and the reliving of a life story, of the ongoing struggle to overcome those tensions, and of bringing the lived and the told stories of her life closer together. The tensions in the relationship between the lived and the told stories and the ongoing making of new relations and new connections within and between these stories was being experienced as "pushes and pulls…as contractions and expansions…as lightness and weight, rising and falling, harmony and discord" (Dewey, 1934, p. 134). At the same time as Anne was feeling the disparities in the expression of the retelling in the context of living, she was also experiencing the ongoing surprises inherent in the reliving, necessitating that they be built into future retellings and thus creating a sense of further tension and of incompleteness.

I can now trace what I understand as a very significant event in the development of my current understandings of the way in which knowledge is reconstructed and of the split between the lived and the told stories of a person's life to an October day in 1987 when I was reading Carr (1986) for the first time. Carr's explanation of the reconstruction of knowledge in musical terms held a powerful and insightful meaning for me then, and it haunted me thereafter, as I often found myself relating it to my readings, discussions, and reflections in and around the topic. Carr (1986) explores the concept in terms of the temporal structures of experience and action that reach back into the past and forward into the future for their meaning. He explains the process of the reconstruction of the whole into a new temporal arrangement by likening the text of our experience to that of a musical score that can sometimes take surprising turns and present us with something other than that which we have expected, leaving us with our expectations unfulfilled.

> When this happens, it has turned out that, in effect, we are not hearing the melody we thought we were. The notes, even the past ones, are now part of a different whole: what they are "heard as" is revised retroactively. Thus many of the temporal wholes whose parts we experience are configurations destined never to be realized and indeed, in a certain sense, configurations which never existed "except in our minds." (Carr, 1986, p. 29)

Our experiences, be they musical or life experiences, exist in time and can be temporal or permanent according to the effect they have on us. They have a past, a present, and an imagined future, and they are dependent for their perception and comprehension upon our abilities to make meaning of what is being experienced in the present, in light of what is remembered from the past and what is predicted for the future. Remembering and predicting are required, and when that which we have predicted takes an unexpected turn, we are taken by surprise. The process of readjustment is that of a reordering of the relations between the components of a new present and a restructured future and past, which now make up a different whole.

Carr's (1986) explanation helped me to understand Anne's experience and to see that through the reliving and retelling of a story for the present, Anne engaged in the questioning of current and past practices and theories, the reordering of relations within and between them, and the restructuring of her personal practical knowledge. The process was one of "turning over" and examining long-held concepts and reconstructing the past in light of the newly constructed present and a tentatively imagined future. Anne's rediscovered voice played out the melodies and rhythms of a new score for her daily life in the classroom, bringing it into a new, coherent, and harmonious unity with her experienced past and imagined future as well as bringing to her life a new sense of professional empowerment and of renewal.

CHAPTER 6

Reconstructing a Narrative

IMAGE, IMAGINATION, AND VOICE
CONNECTED IN INQUIRY

Was music once the proof of God's existence?
As long as it admits things beyond measure,
That supposition stands.

Seamus Heaney, "A Window," 1989

Teaching, Learning, and Telling a New Story of the Self

Anne's new story of the self is the story of an inquiry in which image and imagination provide a framework for the making of new relations and for the restructuring of a narrative within which past, present, and future are woven into a harmonious and coherent unity. This new story was being told in September 1989, at the beginning of Anne's fourth year in the core classroom and the end of our collaborative work in the classroom. The details of the inquiry focus on Anne's ongoing efforts to reconcile the tensions between aspects of her own changing narrative and the narratives of those with whom she was in relation. From the perspective of her fourth year in the core classroom, she looked back and retrospectively told the story of the changes she saw in her own practice.

Anne's story describes the details of the ways in which image and imagination were linked during inquiry and in which imagination mediates "between experience and projected action, employing the same sorts of aesthetic forms for each, making, for instance, a single continuous story out of the experienced past and the willed project" (Crites, 1979, p. 125). Her story tells of the transformation of voice, of her personal practical knowledge, and of the reconstruction of her narrative of herself. It highlights the ways in which Anne brought her own voice and the voices of those with whom she was in relation into a more balanced and harmonious equilibrium where new tensions and inharmonious and irrhythmic incidents could be dealt with within an ever-changing and moving equilibrium. Between its lines, it speaks of discovery, adaptability, and the creativity required to generate new relations and new possibilities, to question, to reflect, and to make a new music. It is told here to throw light on the meaning of professional inquiry and on the details of the process of constructing a new narrative for the self, the fruits of which were professional growth and development. I have drawn on the field notes of September 1989 to tell the story of this making of a new music.

The Making of a Music—Anne's Story

I find it interesting to be looking back now that I am in the fourth year of the change and thinking about the differences in what I do in the classroom. I find myself talking about my classroom teaching in the way I used to talk about what I did in the gym. I have a comfort level with the core classroom situation at last, I feel that teaching is fun for me again, and my old confidence and sense of professionalism have come back. I feel much more confident in my ability to figure out what will work for the students as groups and as individuals, and I have developed a whole range of things that I can draw from. I'm very excited about the kinds of things I see the kids doing. Teaching has become an enjoyable challenge for me again in the way it used to be.

I'm totally involved in an interdisciplinary unit with the class right now, and I am "playing" with it in the way that I used to play with different aspects of the program when I was in the gym. This unit started out in history and English and seems to have expanded to include all the subjects we have together. We began by looking at the stories of conflicts in students' own lives and moved from there into conflicts in current and historical events and in the novels we are reading. The students have choices in their assignments, which are both independent and interdependent, and they are all working both individually and within groups.

Looking back now, I see that I've made considerable changes to the way I do things in the classroom. I find that I'm not tied to the course content in rigid ways, as I used to be when I was less familiar with my situation, and I'm more comfortable with meeting the kids where they need me to help them, by being more flexible and less structured myself. I used to impose so much of the structure on them and wanted to have every last piece of paper nailed down ahead of time so that there was no room for error, but there was no flexibility either. Now I see that they really benefit from doing many of those things themselves, designing some of their own structures and learning by doing, just as I learn better when I

CARL A. RUDISILL LIBRARY
LENOIR-RHYNE COLLEGE

do things for myself. I used to be so hung up on teaching "the basics" and on making them the focus of my teaching, but I see that my teaching is so much more than that now. "The basics" have expanded to include teaching kids to understand the processes of learning and learning how to learn what they need to know, which was something that I had to learn for myself. It seems that everything we read or discuss in one context has applications to so many others. I love working out the connections between subjects, expanding and connecting ideas to one another, and then I get so much satisfaction out of seeing the kids making these connections themselves in really interesting and exciting ways. I want to be able to teach everything in this way, and I'm working on it a bit at a time. I want these kids to be able to hold their own in the different environment of the high school, to have confidence in themselves, and to be capable of finding out what they need to know, to be able to think for themselves and to learn for themselves. This is so much more than knowing "the basics" or having covered the content.

One of the problems I have to face is that many of my new ways of doing things take more time than the way I used to do them. It takes much longer for students to make their own notes on the subject matter of the course as they do now, and for us to discuss what they have done and the process of doing it, than it used to take when I gave them the notes. As a teacher, it is so much easier to do everything yourself and to be tightly organized ahead of time, but I began to see that I was cutting the kids out of a lot of the learning they needed to be doing for themselves, and I knew I had to make some changes. I constantly ask myself what I'm trying to do, and when I remind myself that I'm trying to help these kids to learn how to learn, I know that they have to have a share in the planning and in the processes. It takes more time this way, but the kids are learning more because of it. I realize now that this is more important than covering the content of the curriculum...

I still do SRA [Science Research Associates Reading Lab] at the beginning of each year, and I know that according to the guidelines I should not be using it. I know also that I'm going against the mainstream, but I continue to use it and to like it, because I see benefits to using it that I cannot get in any other way. It is the best way I know to teach the routines and the organizational structures at the beginning of the year, and it gives me the level at which the students are working. The students quickly learn how it is structured and organized; it is marked immediately so that they can see where they are doing well, where they went wrong, and how to make the necessary corrections. These kids come in after school voluntarily to do the SRA, they see progress, and they feel good about it, so I continue to use it. Handwriting practice is another teaching technique that has gone out of style, and yet I think that we have to help kids with this when it is still a problem for them, no matter what grade level we teach at.

When I look back to the beginning now, I realize that it wasn't all new ground as I thought it was then. I did not give myself credit for knowing anything and thought that I had to start from scratch and learn everything I needed to know. I totally underestimated what I already knew, and it has been a slow and gradual realization on my part that I do know something about teaching as a result of all my years of experience, but it has taken time and a lot of effort to adapt it to this new situation. I've had a lot of help from friends and from colleagues, such as Kate, Robbie, and Mary, who came into the classroom and worked directly with the kids and with me. It makes a big difference to me when I have resource help for the kids in the class who need that bit of individual help to do what they are doing and who would be lost without it. It is so good for me to have people to talk to, to share ideas with, and to work things out with. I've always felt that I've made progress and improved my teaching when I have colleagues to work with and we can figure things out for ourselves, adapting and refining them as we see how they work with kids. I have taken on new responsibilities now to help other teachers, and I try to help them in the way that I was helped when I needed it.

I know I'm doing something right when I see how far my kids have come at the end of every year. I always feel that there's so much more that could be done, but I know, too, that they are ready to be successful on their own when they leave me. I'm always delighted when they come back to visit, and I'm sure they do so for many reasons, but when they do come, it says something to me—I'm not sure what—but I'm always intrigued and I think that something must have made an impression on them.

Anne's story tells of the seemingly inexplicable and immeasurable process of the making of a new music. Her voice tells of the living of a new story for the classroom that is true and authentic to herself and to those with whom she is in relation. It tells of her successfully renegotiated relationship with her environment through her efforts to become increasingly more responsive and reciprocal within the relationships of which she is a part, as well as of the achievement of the feelings of stability, of balance, and of harmony she sought, her voice bearing "within itself the germs of a consummation akin to the aesthetic" (Dewey, 1934, p. 15).

Anne's story tells of the ways in which past experiences were used to construct new and better ones for the situation she was living out. Retrospectively, she acknowledges and values the experienced knowledge (Hunt, 1987) that provided the framework for her inquiry and the experiences inherent in the restructuring of that knowledge to meet the needs of the changed environment. This knowledge included a deep understanding of adolescent students; of lesson, unit, and yearly planning; of school routines and cycles of events; of the board and community milieu and of herself as a teacher and learner. Anne can now acknowledge that it was this experienced knowledge that provided the "deep-seated memory of an underlying harmony" (Dewey, 1934, p. 17) that she drew on, that guided and directed the restructuring of her personal practical knowledge and the subsequent restoration of her self-esteem and renewal of her personal energy and enthusiasm for teaching.

The story illustrates the process of one teacher's successful attempts to create an environment of "interactive professionalism" (Fullan, 1991), telling of how she drew on her resources and reconstructed the team-teaching situation she had known in the gym in order to acquire the new knowledge, skills, and strategies that she felt she needed in her new and changed situation. It tells of a commitment to strategies that would benefit students as persons and of providing learning situations that would foster their need to become more autonomous, empowered learners both as individuals and as members of a community. It shows the ways in which the goals identified, the successes and failures assessed, and the professional development planned were inextricably connected to the relational situation within which they were determined and understood. Her story provides insights into the ways in which she dealt with the numerous paradoxes emanating from the ongoing struggle to reconcile the balances between "talking less, so that students can talk more, yet giving students what they need"; "to give away some control in order for students to learn the process of self-control, but to be 'in control'"; "to be more flexible so that students can have the opportunities to design their own frameworks and structures, but not to be unplanned or disorganized"; and "to give and to respond in professional relationships while maintaining something with which to give and to respond in personal relationships." These quotes from Anne, taken from my field notes throughout the research period, reflect a pattern of struggle that runs through her descriptions of her experience of change. Finally, Anne's story tells of an approach to her own inquiry into teaching and learning that is creative, adaptable, and flexible and that highlights both the ethics and the aesthetics of the art of teaching.

Any one story told retrospectively, such as the one told here, by its very form and sequencing of events, gives an impression of linearity and belies the looping, the shifting, and the zigzagging movements and rhythms of growth as it was actually experienced. The ups and downs, the successes and failures, and the backward and forward movement of the journey can only be revealed in the details of the clusters of stories that make up the totality of the experience. The art of teaching and of inquiry into teaching requires constant decision making, judging, and questioning of past and current practices and held theories, values, and beliefs. For Anne, this involved many occasions in which obstacles and resistance were confronted and dealt with within the normal course of a school day. The following piece tells of such an occasion and deals with the overcoming of resistance, showing the details of Anne's struggle to establish her image of family relations in a classroom that students thought of as competitive and independent rather than collaborative and interdependent. It shows, too, the interaction of theory and practice during the process of inquiry and the ways in which they are influencing, shaping, and restructuring each other during that inquiry. I have titled the piece "Responding to the Nigglings," as it is one of Anne's phrases. I once asked her to explain what it meant to her within the context of her teaching, and I draw from my field notes of October 1988 to quote her words here: "I have a big plan that I adapt and work with all the time as I get to know the kids better, but when I make a decision to do something different, as I did the other day, I don't really do things consciously, I just respond to the nigglings. You know, when things are not right and you do something about it, and that's what I call the nigglings."

Responding to the Nigglings

Anne stopped the class midway through the period and proceeded to take a new and unplanned direction. The students had been working in groups of four so that they could help each other to plan the oral presentations of their work on the Olympics, and what we had planned was not working. It was mid-October, the 1988 Olympics were in full swing, and the students had been working on the Olympics unit since early September, progressing through the activities of the unit and making personal scrapbooks to display their work. I had been in the class on several of the days when they worked on the unit and had talked to them about many of the activities and helped them with their work in progress. I wouldn't easily forget the day when Ben Johnson won the gold medal for Canada and was raised to the status of a cult hero, or the day when he was disqualified and all but a few still stood up for him and refused to believe that he had let them down. I wouldn't easily forget the day our planned lesson on "helping each other to plan" had flopped either.

Many times throughout September and October, Anne had expressed regret at having started a unit such as this too early in the year, before the routines and rules of the classroom had been established and before the students were ready to work in groups. Her feelings had been reinforced by the way the particular class she spoke of now had gone. Anne had stopped the proceedings in midstream when the noise level in the room and the interactions between students told us both that the groups were not functioning cooperatively. Many of these students had never spoken to a large group before, and, knowing that they needed help and support to prepare for this, we had planned for them to have an opportunity to rehearse their informal speeches in front of a small group in order to get positive and constructive feedback and to receive help and support from their colleagues in the preparation of the final speech. Our plans had gone awry; some of the students had been doing all the talking, and others would have left the class without having had any opportunity to talk or to express any of the dilemmas they were facing at the future prospect of presenting their work in a public way. Anne had stopped the class and had focused instead on the process of working cooperatively, reminding students of ways they could be helpful to one another and of the importance of equality of opportunity for everyone in the class. After the class was over, she had said to me, "Well, we're behind schedule now because of this unexpected turn of events, but there was no point in going on when they were not helping each as we had planned. I knew that it was more important to stop and talk about what it means to treat each other as human beings than it was to go on with what we had planned. It became increasingly obvious to me that they needed a lot more help with understanding the process of working in small groups than I had originally thought. We've been flexible and adjusted our schedule a few times before, and I guess we'll be doing it again."

During the week that followed, Anne had adjusted her schedule so that the students would get the help they needed and would be ready to begin to make their presentations today, as planned. She did this by coming in early in the morning and staying after school to help them and by giving them feedback as they practiced. I had arrived just in time to see the last flurry of preparations for the presentations that were about to begin. Some of the students looked really nervous as they played with the cards on which they had written the notes they would use, while others looked well prepared and anxious to get started. Anne welcomed me and said, "All of these kids are prepared, but I've made an exception for a few of the students for whom English is a second language, and they are going to make their presentation to me and to a few other students after school next week, instead of doing it in front of the entire class." She then gave me the two typed pages she had used to help them to prepare their speeches and to deliver them when the time came. As I read over them, she said, "I don't know what the quality of these presentations will be like, but I'm really impressed with how these kids have been preparing during spare moments throughout the school day and staying after school to practice."

Anne went to the front of the class and reminded the students that it was time to begin. She pointed to the blackboard, where she had written "Be a kind and sensitive audience," and asked the class to explain to her how they were going to be this kind of audience. As they put their hands up, she called on them individually, and they gave answers such as "By sitting quietly and listening and showing interest," "By asking good questions at the end," "By being patient with any mistakes someone might make and encouraging them to continue," "By asking relevant questions that they might know the answers to," and "By clapping at the end." Anne accepted all these answers, and her responses spoke of pleasure and satisfaction. Then she said, "A good audience is very important to the speaker who is really going through a very difficult time and needs your help." Asking the students to begin then by volunteering their names, she wrote them on the blackboard as they were given, thus providing an agenda for the class. Anne and I then moved to either side of the class, sat down, and prepared for the first speaker.

Zoe was first and she walked up to the front of the class, smiled, and began her speech to an audience who listened attentively, responded, and then asked questions as they had said they would. Anne said, "Zoe, your speech was very well planned and delivered and you seemed very organized. I really liked the way you used the cue cards to help you." Zoe beamed her delight at Anne's response, and then one by one the students went to the front of the room and gave their speeches, all seeming to relax once they began and could see and feel the encouragement and interest being shown by their colleagues. The questions asked had a genuineness to them in that they looked for further information on the content of the speeches or on the process of preparation and presentation. The presenters answered the questions, talked further about the issues, and accepted the responses offered to them, seeming to blossom with the sense of achievement the whole experience was giving them.

I could tell from Anne's comments and the look on her face that she was pleased with the quality of the work being presented, the way in which the students were stretching and challenging themselves to make their presentations and to listen and to respond to one another's work. Her face registered her pleasure every time a student made a positive and constructive comment on another's work, and she, too, gave an appreciative and encouraging comment to every student who presented. To David, she had said, "Your work is excellent, and I know how much time you have spent preparing this speech. Tell us what you learned about yourself through working on it." David replied that he had learned that he needed to be more organized and to plan ahead. Anne agreed with him, looked over at me and smiled, a smile that seemed to say, "And he said it too! . . . I couldn't have said it better myself!" To Laura, who had made a speech about Ben Johnson, disagreeing with his disqualification and giving the reasons for her opinion, Anne said, "Laura, I loved the way you expressed your feelings and opinions about this issue. That took a lot of courage and I congratulate you." To Rahim, who had made a great effort to be understood because his English was tentative, Anne had said, "Rahim, have you ever spoken in front of a group in English before"? Rahim smiled and said that he had not, whereupon Anne's face lit up and, turning to address the whole class, she said, "I think we should give Rahim a special round of applause. This was a very special occasion for him today, and he did very well. Well done, Rahim." Rahim stood there calmly, 14 years old, nearly six feet tall, and proud as could be, accepting the applause, the admiration, and the confirmation of belonging.

At the end of the class Anne spoke to the students and said: "I'm really pleased with what I've seen today. I'm really happy. Those of you who did your work today did a great job, and you should be very proud of yourselves. The volunteer system is working well, and I like it when you volunteer rather than waiting for me to assign you a place." Her face glowed, and I knew then how much it had meant to her to see the students doing so well, to see them helping and supporting one another and genuinely pleased at one another's successes.

This story is set within the context of the first few months of the official change to middle school and of the organizational and program changes this involved. Anne had decided to start the year with an interdisciplinary unit on the Olympics, even though she had to go against her usual practice and held theory in order to do so. She had made her decision on the basis of the need to provide for the wide variety of abilities and needs of the students in this class, and also in order to take advantage of the actual event taking place in Seoul, South Korea, at the time. In September Anne explained her decision to me in this way, and I recorded her words in my field notes:

This class is very different from last year's. I've got a lot of regular grade 8 kids in the class as well as the ESL kids I'm used to, and I've got a lot less structure earlier on in the year because of this. The regular grade 8 kids are much more advanced academically than the kids I've had during the past two years, and I need to provide for this wide variety of abilities I have. With this independent study I can give them the opportunity to work at their own pace and to make their own choices, and I can take advantage of the event too. I've already paired them up, pairing an ESL student with each regular grade 8 student and that's a start....

I continue to encourage them to draw on one another for support and as resources, and I guess I'm showing them lots of different ways to do this. They are not ready for group work yet and what they are doing is quite independent, but they are getting choices and I'm working on having them help each other.

Throughout the unit Anne had wondered, worried, and lived with "the nigglings" regarding many of the issues involved, including whether the pacing, the structures, and the frameworks of the unit were meeting the needs of such a diverse group, whether the regular students were getting enough challenge and the ESL kids enough support and help, and whether the number and the quality of the expected assignments was appropriate. The story shows Anne dealing with what she calls "the nigglings" and what Schwab (1971) refers to as the process of examining educational problems and situations in more than one set of terms. These grade 8 students had been at the bottom of the junior high school in grade 7 a few months before and were now at the top of the middle school. In October, Anne explained the significance of this in terms of what it meant for what took place in the classroom. I have drawn from my field notes of October 1988 for these next two quotes from Anne.

All the grade 8's are difficult this year because of the change to middle school and the loss of some of the privileges they had in the junior high such as night dances, but it has been decided by the grade 8 teachers that I have the toughest class to handle. These kids have been giving trouble to all kinds of people throughout the school, and we have done a lot of talking about reputations and how a bad reputation hurts you. Now we are counting the positive things that happen to us as a class and trying to get the positives to balance the negatives.

Many times she expressed her regret at getting involved in an interdisciplinary unit so early in the year. However, by the end of October, when it was all over, she admitted to being surprised and to having had a change of heart about the entire experience.

> In spite of all I said, now that it is all over I'm really glad I did it because when I look back, I can see that the kids really benefited from it. When I saw the quality of the work they did and the presentations they were giving, I changed my mind! I feel really good about the unit now and know that it was all worth it in spite of not getting the routines sorted out ahead of time as I would usually have done. When I see what I have been seeing for the past few weeks, kids teaching one another, supporting one another, and saying the kinds of things they were saying to one another, I know that I did the right thing. Some of these kids don't need as much structure as I would have provided if I had done things my usual way, and giving them what they already have would be slowing them down. This unit allowed more flexibility and more opportunities to do things their way, and when I really think about it, all I've done is like we used to do in the gym, provide the kids with the opportunities and let them do what they could based on their abilities.

Anne's explanation characterizes the way in which she usually credited the successes of the classroom to her students, delighting in them and underestimating her own role. I had another perspective to offer: I saw a teacher whose knowledge, skills, and abilities were constantly focused on the creation of a classroom setting where students would be valued for themselves, would be treated with respect and caring by those around them, and would feel encouraged to participate in all the classroom activities through which they would learn and grow. The stories of her practice tell this story, and they tell also of the development of Anne's professional knowledge within the context of self and of community.

The stories of Anne's practice present what Dewey (1934) called the "drama where action, feeling and meaning are one," within which the "rhythmic beats of want and fulfilment, pulses of doing and being withheld from doing" are felt, and where the "ebb and flow, systole and diastole...the contrast of lack and fullness, of struggle and achievement and adjustment after irregularity" are lived out (p. 16). Here, too, is the expression of "power that is intense because measured through overcoming resistance" (p. 16), a power which has the potential to transform and through which persons are enabled to give voice and form to their visions.

Restructured Knowing: Knowing as if for the First Time

> We shall not cease from exploration
> And the end of all our exploring
> Will be to arrive where we started
> And know the place for the first time.
>
> (Eliot, 1944, *Four Quartets*, p. 48)

Life grows when a temporary falling out is a transition to a more extensive balance of the energies of the organisms with those of the conditions under which it lives. . . . [When] there is an overcoming of factors of opposition and conflict; there is a transformation of them into differentiated aspects of a higher powered and more significant life. . . . Form is arrived at whenever a stable, even though moving equilibrium, is reached. Wherever there is this coherence there is endurance. Changes interlock and sustain one another. Order is not imposed from without but is made out of harmonious interactions that energies bear to one another. Because it is active (not anything static because foreign to what goes on) order itself develops. It comes to include within its balanced movement a greater variety of changes. (Dewey, 1934, p. 14)

Anne's journey toward the achievement of a more balanced and harmonious equilibrium in her life took place through the continuous process of living and retelling the story of herself, a process of telling and retelling what she was living and becoming that which she told. Anne's stories of change show how her own professional voice became more self-assured, confident, and aware of its own significance over time; they also show her in the process of becoming more responsive to the voices of those with whom she was in relation. Anne described her ongoing involvement in reflection on practice and inquiry as "one of the most natural things in the world for me" and explained how the collegial and cooperative team-teaching environment she had known in the gym provided an environment conducive to reflection, a situation she had now re-created in the classroom. I have quoted Anne's written words here, and have drawn from my field notes of April 1988 in order to do so:

> Thinking over a lesson you have taught, and talking about how the kids responded to it and how you might have done things differently, is one of the most natural things in the world for me. I always go back over what I have done in my mind and make plans for how I will do it next time. This was the beauty of working in the gym and being part of the team arrangement, because you had a colleague to do this with.

Anne's story provides insights into the kind of change that transforms, in that the structures within which she knows herself are changed so that she can never be the same again. It describes the process of inquiry where what is known is extended into new areas and continued into "the undergoing consequences" (Dewey, 1916):

> Mere activity does not constitute experience. It is dispersive, centrifugal, dissipating. Experience as trying involves change, but change is meaningless transition unless it is consciously connected with the return wave of consequences which flow from it.... When an activity is continued into the undergoing of consequences, when the change made by the action is reflected back into a change in us, the mere flux is loaded with significance. We learn something. (p. 139)

As Anne made changes in one area of practice, the consequences of those changes were extended to other areas, where they caused reverberations, questions, uncertainties, and wonderings. I saw and heard her question such issues as "subject matter," "the basics," "social skills," "time management," "control," "structure," and "planning," and make tentative new relations and connections among them, the changes in the relations among things bringing changes in the things themselves. I saw and participated in some of Anne's attempts to move toward the interdisciplinary, connected approach she strove for and away from the step-by-step approach where subject content was taught in a linear and compartmentalized way and where the focus had been on the content of the subject area, skill development, and "the basics." Through the questioning, the exploring, and the expanding of her practice, I saw and heard Anne developing the abilities to hear her own voice and becoming more confident and acknowledging of her own knowing. I quote here from my field notes of a planning session for the mythology unit in December 1988, during which Anne looked over the tentative plan and said: "Well, we have all the things we wanted in here, reading, writing, researching, evaluation, collaborating, listening...etc. The question I'm asking myself now is do we need to have vocabulary and spelling in here like we did in the Olympics unit. I don't want it to be too overwhelming, and they are going to have to learn new vocabulary and spelling to do what we have asked them to do anyway, so I guess I've answered my own question."

Within Anne's developing narrative was a growing awareness of the ways in which the creation of new forms, new relations, and new connections were connected inextricably to reconstructed roles for the teacher, the student, the subject matter, and the classroom as a place for learning. Retrospectively, I can now trace the patterns of her changing understandings of these roles and the process of their reconstruction. I can now see the links between Anne's increasing awareness of the direction of her inquiry and her growing acceptance of the ongoing imbalances, inconsistencies, and ambiguities of the process of reconstruction. Her tentative and developing understandings are articulated here in three separate excerpts from my field notes. The first, which was made early on in our work together in September 1987, voices dissatisfaction with her inability to live out the story she was telling in all areas of her practice. The two following quotes were made during our second year together, in January and April 1989, respectively; they show Anne's acknowledgment of her own success in bringing consistency and coherence to her lived and told story in a wider area of practice.

> In English I accept that the kids go at their own pace and I let them go their own way and I know how to deal with it now. I just haven't figured out how to do that in math yet, but I know that it will come. With math, I wish I could stand up there and teach one lesson, but then I think of Leonard, who doesn't have a clue as to what's going on; then there's Aisha, who doesn't understand what I'm saying in English; and Rahid, who is bored because it is all too slow for him… I'm wondering whether I shouldn't be organizing different learning centers around the room too, a math center, a language center, a science center etc…but I know that I'm just not ready for that yet.

Underlying Anne's expression of dissatisfaction with her program here is the imaginative projecting forward and the tentative construction of other ways of being. Within the same school year, she was to describe the way in which she was bringing the lived and the told story together, and extending them both in the process, in a voice I remember as being full of unconcealed joy and delight:

> In math, I've got students working in pairs to talk about the problems they are solving and I'm finding that it makes a *huge* [Anne's emphasis] difference. They check each other's homework every day in groups now, too (I still keep track in my book), but they are becoming much more accountable for their own work and for each other's work, too. When I think of all that time I used to spend checking and ticking work just to keep the records straight…this time is so much better spent teaching and helping the students individually and then giving them the responsibility for keeping their own records. Kate is doing this, too, with another class, and we

talk about what a great idea it is and wonder why we didn't do this before.

Anne was also extending aspects of the story she told into her science program, confirming to herself the morality and the aesthetics of her ways of knowing and being in the classroom. Her words speak of feelings of personal renewal and self-actualization, which have come through increased responsiveness and reciprocity to those with whom she was in relation, and the effects of which affirmed her feelings of faithfulness to herself and to others.

> In science I've had the students give each other feedback on the oral presentations they did (like we did with them for those presentations they did in English last year), and the kids were great...telling what they had learned from one another, supporting and complimenting one another on the work they each had done. It was so good to hear them and it made me feel very good about myself.
>
> The kids are doing all the work now, and anyone walking into this class would wonder what part I played in all of this! I see great improvement in the way they are working together and in the quality of the work they are doing. They talk to one another about their work, offer one another suggestions and can be quite polite to one another, courteous even.... They give one another credit for ideas, for effort and hard work, and the ESL kids are blossoming. They are really challenging themselves because I guess they feel supported...I just love it when I see kids responding in this way, and it makes me think that I must be doing something right.

Through her inquiry and the overcoming of the obstacles and resistances in her life, Anne comes to a new understanding of herself as a professional and transforms that understanding into new kinds of programs for students where the relationship between knowledge and the knower has changed. Anne comes to understand herself as a curriculum maker in the way that she was in the gym, and theory and practice inform and support each other within a dialectical relationship where she questions and suspends belief in either, when they are seen to be in conflict with her image of family relations. Anne has a rediscovered voice that no longer speaks in "small, insignificant, squeaky" tones of her program in the core classroom, a voice that is confident enough to express doubts, certain enough to express uncertainties, and courageous enough to voice weaknesses. She has the confidence to go against a held theory when she sees it is in the interest of the students to do so, and in June 1989 she and Ben, who was also teaching a grade 8 class, combined their two classes for a unit on novels, regrouping them into heterogeneous groupings except for the top four or five students from each class, who were combined to make one group. In an informal conversation Anne explained her reasoning to me and I have quoted her words here from field notes made in June 1989, a time when Anne was completing her third year in the core classroom.

> We both have some really good kids in our classes who we feel need to be challenged, and we have put them together for this unit. Even though I don't believe in ability grouping, I want to do this because I've not challenged these kids before to see how far they could go by themselves. They've always been helping others, and now I want them to have this opportunity of working together within this unit, which has both independent and interdependent activities, and this has been done quite specifically.

Anne deals increasingly and more confidently with the paradoxes and inconsistencies of change, and she has a growing ability to voice her way of knowing new ways of knowing and to deal with the issues that confront her. The following three excerpts, taken from my field notes, reflect this change and these new ways of knowing, the first and second reflecting a changed way of assessing student learning, and the third, a questioning of the theory handed down by "experts" that conflicts with what she knows from her practice. The first quote is taken from the field notes I made after the presentation that Anne and I co-facilitated for the National Middle School Conference in October 1989. Our research in the classroom was over at this time, but we continued to work together occasionally. The next two quotes were taken from field notes written four months earlier, at the end of our official research period, in June 1989.

> I see definite signs of progress being made slowly by students who are more responsive to one another and less dependent on me...developing self-confidence and helping one another, listening to one another, encouraging one another, and actually beginning to compliment one another when opportunities arise.

> You have to be quite flexible when you have a class that is more than half ESL and new kids are arriving daily, and I am much more flexible now than I used to be. I look for where each kid is at now, and I want to be able to give them credit for the effort and hard work they

have put into a piece of work because I will know how much they put into it.... The kids all did their own personal evaluations, one entitled "What I Learned About Myself from Working on This Unit" and the other "What I Learned About Other People from This Unit." They took these home with the formal evaluations I did on their work.

One of the things I have to think about again next year is the length of units of study. The middle school experts say that units should be very short and that kids of this age should not have to spend long on anything. I'm not sure that I agree with that, because in my experience this is not so, and in the case of the mythology unit, I asked the students if they would have liked to spend more time on it, and they all agreed that the time was too short. This is the kind of feedback that helps me to make future decisions, so I will continue to think about this one.

Anne's stories of professional growth describe the details of what takes place during inquiry, when the continuity and discontinuity between that which she has experienced is reflected upon and the imagination links past experiences to future actions. They reveal the ways in which the sense of the aesthetic is ever-present and provides the impetus for further inquiry, showing how Anne achieves the personal and professional satisfactions she does from her ongoing inquiry. Anne assesses her rewards within a relational context and feels them in her successful contacts with students and in the emotional intensity she feels when she influences one of them. She knows and acknowledges success when she sees students influencing one another in progressive and constructive ways as well as when she sees them achieving personal successes due in part to her increased knowledge and skills and to her attainment of the increased levels of "fidelity" (Noddings, 1986) that she has sought for herself.

Through experience and the reflection on experience during inquiry, Anne entered into a process of imaginative questing for hidden but intuited realities, a questing that was structured and understood through her images and given purpose and direction by the tensions created by those images. The process of the reconstruction of her story was bound up with her interactions with others and with the environment in profoundly personal and intimate ways. Hearing her story told back to her by colleagues, who increasingly asked her for help and support, provided echoes and strains of possible new stories that she might begin to tell and that also influenced the process of that reconstruction. Anne's new sense of competence, coherence, and confidence empowered her to take on new challenges and to deal with the ongoing dilemmas of her life as she continually made and remade a world within which shared meanings could be constructed during the interaction of narratives. Anne understands her successes and achievements in a relational sense, and she understands her own growth, self-actualization, and professional development within the context of her ability to respond to those with whom she is in relation in her classroom and her community, through the creation of environments of interdependence and through the empowerment of others.

CHAPTER 7

Collaborating to Learn

A COLLEGIAL PARTNERSHIP
OF CONSULTANT/RESEARCHER
AND TEACHER/PARTICIPANT

> "No man is an island, entire of itself," said
> John Donne in the eighteenth century
> Forgetting to mention those women who
> have lived it all along…
> Knowing themselves and others as "a piece
> of the continent, A part of the main"…
> And me, wondering if I'll ever really understand.
> Mary Beattie, "Relationship," December 1990

Collaborative Partnerships: Purpose, Choice, Trust, and Respect

The purpose of this chapter is to present the story of a collaborative partnership between two experienced teachers—one a consultant/researcher and the other a teacher/participant within this research study—and to describe the establishment and growth of this partnership within the context of studies of reflective practice, professional knowledge, and educational reform. Reviewing the wide range of experiences that Anne and I shared, I have looked for the significant incidents and patterns between and among incidents in order to story the details of the negotiation and establishment of our collaborative partnership for both professional and research purposes and of the establishment of the trust, respect, and reciprocity that was felt and lived out within that partnership. Through stories of collaborative practice, I will show how our individual images became intertwined through the creation of a shared text for collaboration, the process of which became a situation of inquiry and of professional development for each of us.

The lived experience of the establishment of the relationship was different for Anne and for me because of our previous experiences, understandings, and images of practice, yet compressed within each of us were those past experiences and interpersonal relationships that had influenced us and that were now influencing our expectations and forward projections for the relationship we were entering. As Dewey (1934) points out:

> What is retained from the past is embedded within what is now perceived and so embedded that, by its compression there, it forces the mind to stretch forward to what is coming. The more there is compressed from the continuous series of prior perceptions, the richer the present perception and the more intense the forward impulsion. (p. 182)

In deciding to work together, Anne and I had chosen each other from among other possible partners, choosing also the ways in which we would work together and co-designing a working situation that would address our shared interests in teaching and learning and the different purposes for which we had entered into the relationship. In the stories we each tell about the beginnings of our relationship, we have talked of "not knowing what to expect," yet as we negotiated our possible relationship, we had both talked of the importance of trust, respect, and equality in a partnership, and of the creation of an atmosphere within which shared and opposing understandings could be discussed and lived with. We each talked of the need for agreement and argument, discussion and dissention, and the collaborative negotiation of meaning. Retrospectively, we each spoke of the importance of choice and of having chosen each other from among possible others, because of an initial trust and attraction to the other and the expected fulfillment of individual and shared purposes in our collaboration, each valuing what we could learn from the other and feeling that we had something of value to give to the other in return.

During the first class in which Anne and I worked together in her classroom, we both helped individual students with a previously assigned project that they were working on independently. We moved around the room responding to requests from some students and looking to see if anyone was having difficulties. As I was finishing up with one student, Anne asked me if I would give some help to Aisha, a student whose lack of proficiency in English prevented her from moving forward with the assignment. I thought nothing of the request at the time or the way in which it was phrased, but after the class was over, Anne asked me if I had minded being asked to help Aisha, adding that she thought that she might have been a bit brusque because she was so busy in the middle of the class. "I hope I don't overwhelm you," she said, "because I'm so used to working in a team in the gym that I'm inclined to be a bit bossy, and I wouldn't want you to take it the wrong way." She smiled as she said this and looked at me to see how I would take it. I still remember the sense of relief I felt at this open invitation to react to a way of working together that we had discussed but were now living out in the classroom, and I remember my response well. I said, "I think this is great, because I'm inclined to be a bit that way myself, so we may be just perfectly suited to each other." We both laughed, and it seemed that an invisible bond had been established between us and that we had taken the first steps toward establishing the open, honest, equal relationship we had each said we wanted and could now feel was really possible.

As I look back now at the beginnings of our relationship, I am reminded of the feelings of welcome and comfort I felt as soon as I began to work with Anne in her classroom. As a newcomer to her classroom, she quickly made me feel that we were "in things together" and that she valued me as another teacher in the room. Her sincere and straightforward approach, as outlined in this story of the first day of our working together, alleviated the anxiety I was feeling in a way that surprised and delighted me, made me feel that I could be myself within this relationship and that we would each be able to maintain our individual differences and integrity within this collaborative partnership. Later on, when I realized how important it was for Anne that students should feel a strong sense of belonging to the class and I saw her practice in terms of her image of family relations, I came to understand these early days within this context. Having agreed to work with me, she now considered me one of the family, and our roles would be defined by this image. To Anne, our partnership was one in which we would look out for each other, would begin to try to understand each other, and would respect and be responsive to each other's needs.

In my search for a participant in the research study, I had hoped to establish an equal partnership with a teacher in which we would both learn and grow as professionals. I was interested in looking at the meaning and the process of change as it was experienced from the teacher's perspective, and I was willing to work with my participant in her classroom in ways that she would determine. Having spoken to a number of teachers in the inservice project, all of whom were experiencing the process of change, about the possibility of collaboration for research purposes, Anne became my first choice because of her ongoing experiences with the change that she had voluntarily initiated and because of her manner, her personality, and her enthusiasm for the proposed project. I felt drawn to her very quickly because of her open acknowledgment of the value she saw for herself in the collaboration and because I felt that the partnership would provide opportunities through which we would learn from each other.

As a researcher/consultant/teacher, I had entered this relationship with certain expectations regarding our collaboration but without any real plotline for how I would live out my part as either researcher, consultant, or teacher or for the part I had agreed to, wherein these roles were to be combined. Once again, I was on a journey without a road map and trying to feel comfortable with the uncertainty that lay ahead. I was anxious about being a consultant, which I felt could be a disadvantage to me in my efforts to work within equal partnerships with teachers, who might now see me as "someone from the board," and about my lack of an imaginative framework or model for the kind of consulting role I hoped to create. At this time I was also conscious of the ongoing struggle between control and creativity in my life, and I wondered how this would be lived out within the context of my relationship with Anne and my relationships with the other teachers in the inservice context as well as within the context of a collaborative research study.

Within my relationship with Anne, I was to experience a sense of connectedness, commitment, and interdependence that I had only previously experienced within the context of long-term, personal relationships. I was to come to new understandings about what it meant to be a teacher, a consultant, and a researcher and to have the boundaries of my understandings of professional partnerships and collaboration pushed forward to new levels of knowing. The initial feelings of trust and respect that we had for each other were to develop into the reflexivity, responsiveness, and reciprocality of a mutually adaptive interpersonal relationship (Hunt, 1987), through which we both learned and grew as professionals. Anne talks about the beginnings of our relationship as "so easy," yet from my perspective they were tense and uneasy until I could enjoy the sense of relief when our collaboration was agreed upon and we began to plan how we would work together. Anne talks about feeling that she knew me before she met me, because of what Carol had told her, and feeling that she could trust me because she trusted Carol. She explained this to me in May 1989 as we were drawing close to the end of our work together, and I have drawn from my field notes of that time to quote her words here:

> I was nervous of you in the beginning because you know so much and I so little about this core [classroom] situation. However, that first day when you came in and mixed in with the kids, interested in everything and truly interested in the kids, I just knew that things would be OK. As time went on and we played with things together and laughed together…knowing that I could look at you over the kids' heads, raise my eyebrows and you would know what I was saying…. Then I knew that our relationship was a good one, and I started to realize, too, that we were driving each other just the way Carol and I used to drive each other in the old days and the way Ben and I are now.

When Anne tells the story of our collaboration, she does so within the context of a career in which close, collaborative relationships have been a part of her life; her image of family relations structures the ways in which she understands and lives within her world. Looking back at this time now, I see that it was Anne's image of family relations and her previous experiences with professional partnerships that provided the framework for our work together and for the ways in which we structured our current and future practices. I have used Anne's terms—*trust, respect, equality,* and *valuing*—to present the story of that collaboration. In the following piece I tell the story of the establishment of our collaborative partnership in Anne's voice, and it provides insights into the details of the imaginative structures that her image of family relations provided for us as we worked together. I have drawn from my field notes of June 1989, at the end of our research relationship, to present the story of our collaborative partnership.

Professional Partnerships

I was really interested in getting your help in the classroom, and I didn't think much further than that at the time. The benefits all seemed to be so one-sided and weighted in my favor, and at the beginning, I often wondered if you were getting enough out of the arrangement for the amount you were putting into it. I could never really understand this, but I always knew that you would be honest with me, too, if you were not getting what you needed for the research.

Our relationship was one of the four close professional partnerships that I have been lucky enough to have had during my teaching career, and these relationships have been a very special part of my teaching life. I have had many other kinds of professional relationships with colleagues, where we worked and taught together and collaborated at different levels, but I have had four very close relationships where we shared so much of ourselves and had so much invested in the relationship that we learned a lot from each other and became part of each other's lives. Our relationship was one of those, and I think it is important to say that in every one of them, I entered into the relationship by choice. I strongly believe that you can only build this special kind of situation with certain trusted colleagues, so the choice aspect is a critical one. In every case, there has been a high level of respect, of trust, and of dependence on the other, and I have always felt free to argue and to disagree when this is important to me and to work through the little conflicts that come up from time to time without letting them get in the way. We always had our incidents of conflict and disagreement, but we worked through them and came closer together because of them, always talking things over to-gether and making decisions collaboratively. I believe that it is in this way that you develop the closeness, the trust, and the dependence on each other that is so important.

In our work together, I've always done things my way, and you've helped me in the ways I chose, and this is very important. At the begin-ning, I wanted to learn about writing process, as I was feeling pressure to know about it at this time, and I did not want to take the after-school in-service as I was already overloaded and could not manage any more. Very early on, you made me feel that you would help me to manage that load, that we would enjoy working together, and that you would help me in the ways I chose. Once I got to know you and to trust you, I did not hesitate to ask for the help and support I needed, and I valued the wealth of ideas, your years of classroom experience, and the background knowledge that you brought to the classroom. I really appreciated the flexibility of your approach and the great capacity for resourcefulness and adaptability you have. We were always equals in whatever we did, and you valued my ideas, my ways of doing things, and my suggestions and feedback. There was an equality, a sharing, a deep level of trust, re-spect, and commitment on both sides, and I don't think that our rela-tionship could have developed the way it did otherwise.

Building on Trust and Respect: Toward Understanding and Valuing

As Anne and I worked together and our relationship developed, we talked increasingly about the process of our collaboration, talking about the aspects of the relationship from which we each saw ourselves benefit-ing and openly acknowledging the value of each other's strengths and ways of knowing. We built on the initial trust and respect we had for each other and moved toward a greater understanding of the other and a greater valuing of each other as collaborative partners. We often talked about that tacit but previously unarticulated knowledge we both held, shared our tentative understandings, and became participants in each other's stories. We each influenced the ways in which the other imagined the future and told new stories of herself within that future. We shared our successes and failures, the similarities and differences in the way we understood things, and other ways in which we might have understood. Sometimes we came to understand in new ways because of the insights and perspectives offered by the other.

We shared stories that came closer and closer to the central issues of our lives and to the struggles we were both experiencing with reconciling the conflicting aspects of our personal narratives. In sharing our stories we continued to form and to re-form ourselves and the collaborative relationship we were living out. My respect for Anne's teaching grew as I saw how closely that teaching responded to "doing what is right for the students" and to the shared purposes of those with whom she was in relation. In watching the way she responded to others, I saw her efforts to enter into the other's understanding and to see things from the other's perspective. I saw, too, that she was showing me new ways to think about myself as a teacher, a consultant, and a researcher. I saw and heard Anne begin to tell new stories of herself as a teacher, and I heard her being storied in new ways by colleagues. I also began to tell new stories of myself as a teacher, a consultant, and researcher, and the story of collaboration that I tell here is one of working in an exciting, emotional, educative situation. I felt that my ongoing struggle with control and creativity was being lived out in ways that were very positive, creative, innovative, and highly satisfying to me. I also felt that through our improvising and playing together, I was learning, changing, and growing.

Playing Together: Improvising on a Theme

When I arrived at Anne's classroom at the beginning of each lesson, she would quickly describe the plan and outline the roles we would each play within the scenario she envisioned. As she did so, I would feel the excitement of being a part of this lovely, creative, flexible approach and feel the joy of collaborating, of improvising together, and of living out what we were to co-create as we lived it. Walking toward her classroom, I always wondered what lay in store, knowing what we had planned but knowing, too, that Anne would have adapted, modified, and rearranged our tentative plans. I knew that the lesson we would co-teach would be one that would take into account the various needs of the very diverse groups of students in the class as they had emerged and changed since we had done the planning. I looked forward to seeing what she had made of our combined ideas and to being a part of living it out in the classroom.

Anne often used the words *playing together* to describe what we did when we collaborated, and I described it as *finding the music*. I thought of us as two musicians without a score, improvising around a theme which we had identified and within which we played, taking turns to make our voices heard, picking up phrases and rhythms from each other, and joining together to play in unison in a melody that emerged as we created it. Our work reminded me of happy times when I played in school orchestras and chamber groups and sang in choirs. We often talked about this and reminded each other how good it was to have someone to play with.

I have come to understand Anne's teaching now in terms of her image of family relations. Then I described it to myself as responsiveness to others, a very special kind of listening, and the creation of a classroom environment where students would look out for one another, understand one another and like one another, as they learned the subject matter of the courses and the processes of learning how to learn. I could see that Anne's sense of satisfaction and professional self-esteem was influenced by the extent to which she felt she was responding to students and helping them to respond to one another. My growing understandings had the effect of drawing me closer to her and making me feel an increasing sense of wanting to help and support her and become an increasingly more valuable partner to her. I knew that I could do this by listening, by entering into her understandings more fully, and by stretching my own capacities to respond to her as I saw her doing with students and with me. My efforts to do so seemed to strengthen the feelings of value, trust, and respect that had initiated the actions in the first place and to draw us even closer together.

As I look back now, I can see that the satisfaction and enjoyment we both felt in working together grew as we each saw the influence we were having on the other and the ways in which our individual stories were being woven together in a shared text within which we were each restorying our individual stories. We talked about these things during our work together and grew to recognize that valuing and the expression of that valuing seemed to create the conditions and the impetus to be of increased value for each of us. In Anne's words, we "drove each other." When our collaboration was over and we talked about it all, Anne described what for her were the most valuable aspects of the relationship. I have presented what she described in the following piece, drawing on my field notes written at the end of our research relationship in June 1989.

Valuing Within Relationship

I found it very valuable to have you there with me in the classroom, as we could respond to situations together and afterwards could discuss the unexpected turns that had taken place. I could look across the classroom at you and give you a look or a smile and know that you knew what I was talking about and that we could pick up on it later. I could talk to you about things that had happened between your visits, and it was great for me to be able to get responses from someone who knew exactly what I was talking about and could understand the situation without my having to explain it at great length. You really listen to what I say, and I can talk to you as a colleague and as a friend.

One of the things that I did not expect from our collaboration was that in all the talking I've done to you about myself as a teacher, I've come to a better understanding of what it is that I can do, and I am more capable of expressing this for myself now. Our conversations, collaborative planning, and team teaching have helped me to think about what I do know about teaching and about students and to be able to relate what I knew from my days in the gym to the classroom situation. Together we took on challenges that I would not have taken on my own, and together we could do what neither of us could have done alone. Sharing ideas and talking about my concerns has certainly helped me to develop my knowledge and skills and the confidence level that goes along with this.

When I read what you had written during the summer at the end of our first year of work together, I was amazed at how much you had understood about the way I see things in the classroom. You described my beliefs and the things that are important to me but which I had never said in words, and as I read those "Images of Practice," I felt that I was seeing myself on paper. I remember thinking, and then saying to you later on, "There's so much of me in this that it is frightening." It is still frightening, but it is also fulfilling.

From my perspective, the developing relationship was providing me with a rich learning environment in which the details of my personal narrative and the shared text we had created were being lived out together. From Anne, I was learning how to listen to the voices of others in new ways; to suspend my own judgments, opinions, and understandings in order to enter into those of others; and then to return and to understand aspects of my own personal practical knowledge in new ways—learning what it feels like to depend and to be depended upon, to give and to receive, to trust and to be trusted, to value and to be valued. The classes we taught seemed to reflect the closeness of collaboration that we had established, and I felt that we experienced our rewards from the responses of the students and from our responses to each other. I can best describe the rewards I felt and the felt meaning of being valued and respected within a professional relationship by relating the story of an incident that took place at the end of our second year of work together. This was a very powerful and moving experience for me at the time, and I believe that the emotions I felt then have colored my subsequent collaborative attempts. I have attempted to present the felt qualities of the experience in this next piece, drawn from my field notes of May 1989.

Professional Development Through Interacting Narratives

In the face of a swiftly approaching deadline, Anne and I had worked together for two periods helping students to write stories, anecdotes, chants, and poems for the school yearbook. The lesson itself had been quickly prepared, and we had planned, prepared, and taught together, straining our mutual capacities for creativity and adaptability to the limit. We both felt all the anxieties associated with the possibility that we might not be successful and that the students' work would be omitted from the yearbook in spite of our efforts.

The students responded with work that surpassed our wildest expectations and were themselves delighted with what they had produced. Afterwards, when we were both sitting in the seminar room feeling drained, Anne was looking through the students' work, and she suddenly put the papers down and looked at me, her eyes all misted up, and said, "You'll never know what you've done for me today." I felt the full meaning of her words and the profound satisfaction that comes from knowing that we had truly made this happen together.

Creating a Shared Text: Interacting Narratives

In a relationship that we each describe as successful and beneficial both personally and professionally, there were times when the interaction of two people who are in the world differently produced tensions, frustrations, and misunderstandings. In the two years we worked together, we never did have a situation that I would describe as a conflict, even though there were many times when our different understandings became evident and were brought out and discussed. Several months after the official research period was over, Anne was describing our relationship within the context of the other professional relationships of which she was a part, and I have drawn from my own journal of October 1989 to quote Anne's words here.

> In most close relationships, there are usually some times of conflict, but we never did have any conflict in all the time we worked together, which I think is unusual. I believe that it was because we talked so much about everything, and misunderstandings just never got a

chance to arise. We may have lacked conflict, but we didn't lack laughter, and I do remember that we laughed a lot. I really enjoyed the fun we had, and I miss that now, as I miss having you to talk to on such a regular basis.

Looking back over our relationship, I, too, believe that through honest and open communication we dealt with our different understandings as they arose, and then we moved on. I have chosen to tell two stories here that I think of as "difficult" incidents in our relationship; the first is called "Holding Back and Reaching Out" and the second, "Changing Roles— Holding Back and Reaching Out." These two stories tell of times when our conflicting understandings of the situation caused friction, frustration, and anxiety; they describe experiences that show the working out of those tensions, the creation of new understandings, and the opening up of new collaborative possibilities. Each story gives insights into the ways in which the boundaries of a relationship that has been built on the understanding of individual integrity and individual strengths within a shared and equally balanced unity are tested and explored. Each story shows, too, the struggle for voice and for imaginative control on the part of one partner in the relationship and the corresponding struggle on the part of the other to hear and understand that voice in order to participate in the imaginative situation being described. I have drawn from my field notes of February 1988 for the details of the incident recounted here, when Anne and I had been working together for six months.

Holding Back and Reaching Out

It was the end of the school day, and Anne and I had worked with the class all afternoon. I was anxious to make our usual discussion and planning session as short as possible, because I was feeling symptoms that I believed forecast the onset of flu. I felt inordinately tired and lethargic and had the beginnings of a headache. I was dreading the thought of the two or three hours of work I still had to do before I could give in to these feelings. My field notes could not wait; they had to be done while they were still fresh in my mind, and I was anxious to get home, get them done, and bring this day to a close.

Anne began to talk about the novel study unit that she wanted to start with students as soon as possible, and my heart sank as I heard her talk about how much she wanted to do some serious planning on it before we went home that evening. I thought about how difficult it was going to be for me to be creative and enthusiastic when I was feeling so dull and uninspired, and I wanted to leave the novel study until we met later that week. Slowly, as I started to feel that Anne really wanted to work on the unit right then and there, I felt nervous at the thought of doing the things that normally came so easily when we worked together but that would be a challenge for me at this time.

We began by building on the unit that Anne had used the previous year and that she offered as a starting point. We then continued, as we usually did, by sharing ideas backwards and forwards, by accepting and building on each other's suggestions, and by adapting, modifying, and expanding on the emerging structure that we were co-creating. I was glad to be able to make some useful contributions and to hold up my end of the partnership. After we had worked for about an hour, we both expressed satisfaction with the tentative product we had in place and agreed that it would give students many opportunities for working both collaboratively and independently. We also acknowledged that the activities would provide for increased student choice, control, and accountability over those activities outlined in the unit from the previous year.

I was happy with what we had achieved and glad that I had been able to play my part and to listen and respond to Anne's needs in spite of my feelings. I assumed that we would pick up from where we left off later in the week, but as I began to collect my papers together and to prepare to leave, I had a growing sense that my actions were premature and that Anne wanted to continue. I waited, and Anne talked about really wanting to choose the novels for the unit before we left. I wondered out loud if we might wait until the next day to do this, but Anne seemed quite certain that she wanted to do it then and not later. Choosing novels for the unit involved going to the stockroom and picking out from the available novel sets those that related to our unit, then assessing them in terms of readability and student interest, and finally choosing those we would use.

The stockroom was locked when we got there, but Anne found a caretaker to unlock it, and we began to look through the books, talking about the ones we knew and exchanging ideas and suggestions about their suitability for the different groups we had planned. I was feeling frustrated because I knew how much Anne wanted to make some final decisions, but I could not understand why she could expect to do so without spending a lot of time on it, and it was already so late in the evening. I did not understand why it was so important to get this done before we left. I could literally feel the tension growing between us and getting stronger as time went on and final decisions were not being made. We were finding that there weren't enough suitable novels to meet our requirements among those we recognized, but we continued to look through the books, skimming them, making observations, and suggesting possibilities. I felt that we were "on the horns of a dilemma" and didn't know how it could be resolved, but I reminded myself to have patience, to wait and see how it would all work out, and to be supportive and helpful rather than controlling and decisive.

We made a few tentative decisions regarding four possible novels we could use, and at about six o'clock, having identified a few potential novels that we would each take away and take a closer look at, Anne said, "There's enough here to get started, so let's leave the rest for another day when we aren't so tired." She expressed a real sense of relief at having got this far and thanked me sincerely, saying, "I know that you aren't feeling great, and I really appreciate your help here. I needed you with me because I knew that you would know more of these books than I would. Thank you so much for helping me. By the time we meet again, I will have fleshed out the outline in greater detail using these novels we've identified here, and then we can pick up from there. I feel really good about this, and I can't thank you enough."

I was a bit taken aback at the strength of Anne's expression of gratitude, and it was only then that I realized how important the entire incident was to her. I felt relieved that I had acted as I had and had gone along with what she had wanted to do even though I did not really understand what this was or why it was important to do so. Her open expression of gratitude made me glad that I had held back my own feelings, opinions, and lack of understanding and had waited and listened. The event seemed to be one that was rich in meaning for me, and I described it in detail in my field notes, somehow aware of its significance and its importance for me as a learner.

I tell this story here because it has stood out in my mind as an incident that I felt tested the relationship that Anne and I had established and because it was one where I feel that I learned a lot about collaboration from Anne. It tells of the testing of my publicly stated desire to be a better listener and to enter into the understanding of the other in a relationship, and this took place under conditions that I understood as very difficult ones. In the writing of the story I can still recall the feelings I had at the time, feelings of frustration, confusion, and a lack of control as well as the feelings of pleasure and relief I felt when I realized how much it had meant to Anne. As I gained distance from the event and began to see it from new perspectives, I saw that the incident was a highly significant one for me in the development of my understanding of professional relationships.

I now understand this incident within the context of our collaborative relationship, as Anne's attempt to make her voice heard and to live out her story and of my attempts, reluctant though they were, to enter into her understanding and to withhold my voice so that her voice could be heard. I now also understand the incident within the context of Anne's image of family relations and of her struggle to act and to live out her life within the framework of this understanding. I also understand it retrospectively within the context of my ongoing struggle with control and creativity and of my ongoing attempt to know the balance between them in new ways, by learning how to listen to the story of the other in a professional relationship and to construct a shared story in integrated voices. At the time, the situation seemed to me to be unstructured and directionless, and now I see that it was my urge to impose my structures and understandings on it that initially prevented me from hearing Anne's voice and from understanding her structures and her understandings. I remember that in the midst of what I was experiencing as a frustrating and confusing situation, I was conducting an inner rehearsal of the ways in which I would organize and structure the planning if I could do it my way. In the retelling, I recall that it was Anne's persistence that triggered the inner dialogue that reminded me of my publicly stated desire to increase my ability to listen and to be responsive within my professional relationships. At this time, I had documented in my journal several successful incidents of listening and responding within relationships and had begun to think of myself as someone who was becoming successful as a consultant. I knew that I was failing to live out this reconstructed story of myself in this particular situation, and I gradually came to realize it through Anne, who was acting toward me in the way I should have been acting myself. Anne was trusting me and depending on me to listen and to respond, and luckily I was able to realize this in time to do something about it.

Gradually, I put my own story aside and tried to enter into Anne's understandings, touched by the way in which she had continued to trust, to depend, and to ask for the help she needed in spite of my reluctance. Her sincere and open acknowledgment of our partnership, and of the shared ownership and shared responsibility we had in the situation, made a strong impression on me. Afterwards, her expression of gratitude touched me deeply and made me feel right there the joy of holding back my own voice in order to allow the voice of the other to be heard, of struggling to know the world from the other person's perspective, and of the intimate satisfactions to be experienced from the successful outcomes of such a struggle. For Anne, I believe that the incident was understood in the context of her narrative of family relations, where, within our relationship of shared responsibility and shared ownership, we worked as a team.

The second story describes a similar incident where two narrative constructs are in evidence but where the struggle to tell a shared story results in reversed roles for Anne and me. In this incident, it was Anne who struggled to enter my understandings and to live out a role she did not understand. This incident took place toward the end of our two-year research period and is set within a trusting and caring relationship that allowed us to take the kinds of risks and challenges described here and to grow and develop as professionals. The story tells of the follow-up to a planning session in which we had agreed to address Anne's objective of "providing students with increased opportunities for problem solving and decision making," and to do so by teaching the students how to make an oral presentation and to design an evaluation sheet for their own upcoming presentations. I have drawn from my field notes of May 1989 to write this story.

Changing Roles—Holding Back and Reaching Out

Anne and I had decided to co-teach a lesson in which students would identify the criteria of successful oral presentations and use them to design an evaluation sheet for their upcoming oral presentations. This was a challenging situation, as the second part of our lesson depended on the results of the first half. Anne was uncomfortable with the risk factor involved in a lesson where a predetermined sequence of stress could not be followed from beginning to end. She had agreed to try it, as it provided students with opportunities for more direct involvement in the lesson and with insights into the processes of their own learning, thereby responding to the directives of guidelines and of board and school policies. We planned several options for the second part of the lesson based on what we expected to happen in the first half. Our plan was to have small groups of students generate criteria for a successful oral presentation before coming together as a large group to design an evaluation sheet, which students would then use to assess one another's presentations at a later date.

When we were about to begin the lesson, Anne acknowledged that she still agreed to do as we had planned but that she was feeling anxious and nervous about it now that the time to do it was upon us! I knew that she was putting a lot of trust in me, but I was not nervous at all, as I had often taught this way in my own classroom and knew that we could solve whatever problems arose from the risks we were taking. I took my half of the class into the seminar room and Anne stayed in the classroom with her group. We could each see what was going on in the other group, as could the students, who openly listened in and borrowed from the other group's work. Anne and I smiled at each other through the window, knowing what was going on and loving it. The cross-fertilization of ideas was enhancing what we were both doing; the lesson seemed to be a great success and we were all enjoying it. Little did we know that the next part, where we would come together as a large group to share our findings and to design the evaluation sheet, would be such a different story. It was a situation that was to be a challenging and fruitful experience for all of us.

Having come together as a large group, Anne and I decided that she would direct the discussion and I would record everything on the blackboard, but right from the start, everything seemed to go wrong. The students were having trouble differentiating between the characteristics of a good presentation, which they had generated in their small groups, and the actual items to be written down on an evaluation sheet. Their confusion confused us, and we could both feel the sense of frustration building up around us as we recognized the dilemma presenting itself. We had not prepared anything to deal with this eventuality, as neither of us had predicted it. We looked at each other as if to say "What do we do now?"—the looks acknowledging the difficulties we each felt and our sense of confusion about what to do. The public nature of it all was daunting, and we both knew that we were in a dilemma that neither of us knew how to solve. We continued to look at each other, each of us waiting for the other to speak, for what seemed to be an interminable length of time. The silence that had descended on the class was deafening, and I became increasingly aware of the intensity of the students' interest in what was going on, as they looked from one to the other of us, not wanting to miss anything.

Suddenly, we both started to talk at the same time, one of us stopped, and then we were talking to each other about the best thing to do, backwards and forwards, discussing and sharing as we were so used to doing in our planning sessions, but now we were doing it in public with 35 pairs of eyes going backwards and forwards as we talked. Talking and listening, questioning and speculating; it was as if we were in the seminar room after school and we were working on our plans for the next day. We slipped into our usual pattern of planning and worked as we had worked out issues many times before, dealing with this dilemma as we had dealt with so many like it before, but now with the students watching us as if we were characters on a stage in an intense drama. As I became aware of what was going on, I felt a pressure that I thought could only be surpassed by what Anne was feeling, given that she was the classroom teacher and that she was even more exposed than I was. I desperately wanted us to be able to work this out successfully because of all we had at stake and particularly because of what Anne had risked in order to achieve the results we both wanted for the students.

Anne took the initiative and asked the students to work in small groups of three or four, focusing on the classification of the criteria we had identified in the original small groups and on ranking them in order of importance within their classes. As they moved their chairs and started to talk, I remember heaving a huge sigh of relief, looking at Anne and smiling, both of us acknowledging what we had been through and the relief we were feeling that we had worked it through satisfactorily. After the class was over, we talked about it all, and Anne pointed out that in spite of the fact that we would never have planned it this way and would never go through an experience like this on purpose, it had actually provided a great opportunity for the students to see us working collaboratively to solve a problem, dealing with our confusion calmly, and successfully reaching a conclusion. She pointed out that we had modeled the process of cooperation for them and that this was so valuable for them to be able to see, as it was so much the focus of what she wanted them to do in their work together. We laughed at the way they had been so mesmerized and the way the silence had descended on the room when we wanted it least. It was then that Anne admitted that when she had woken up that morning, the first thing she had thought of was this class and of what we had planned to do. She explained that she had felt extremely nervous about it and wondered if the results would be worth the risks we were planning to take. She also said that she had been prepared to do it because we were doing it together and because of the benefits she perceived that it held for students if we should be successful. We acknowledged then that the dual focus of the class introduced too much complexity and that we should have dealt with the material in two lessons rather than one. Anne had solved our problem by recognizing this and by having the students concentrate on acquiring a deeper understanding of the criteria for a successful presentation before they were asked to apply their understandings in the creation of an evaluation sheet.

The next day I went in, Anne showed me the evaluation sheets the students had designed in the following class and were going to use when the presentations started the following week. Her face showed her pride in the students and in the quality of this work they had done. Looking at me then, she shook your head and said, "I wouldn't have done it without you. I've told you before that my life has never been the same since I met you, and now I'm telling you again." I listened and I felt enormous satisfaction because I knew that she really meant what she said. She had trusted me so completely and had taken a huge risk, believing that any difficulties we ran into, we would work out between us. I felt a strong sense of being trusted, depended upon, respected, and rewarded, and I knew that the experience had brought us closer together both personally and professionally.

I tell this story here because it shows the interaction of our narratives through the details of a collaborative experience that was a rich learning situation both for us and for our students. It gives insights into the ways and means through which both Anne and I learned to tell the stories of ourselves in new ways and to bring about changes in our understandings of teaching and learning. The story highlights Anne's understanding of herself within a narrative of family relations, of her ability to listen and to enter into the story of the other and to collaborate in the creation of a shared story. It shows again the ways in which her image of family relations influences her practice and through which she makes new connections and relations between the elements of that which she knows and that which she can come to know in new ways. Reflecting later on this experience and on the various ways in which both she and the students had responded to it, Anne storied and restoried her understandings of structure, of organization, of planning, and of student learning, making new connections and relations among them to tell a new story of herself as a teacher.

The experience of writing about the incident bought back the emotions and the feelings of the original lived experience for me, reminding me again of what it feels like to live in the kind of professional relationship that Anne and I had then and that I always hope to re-create in my ongoing teaching situations. Anne's responses to the students' responses to the lesson touched me in significant ways, causing me to reflect on my own teaching and on my role within personal and professional relationships. I was proud that I had been able to help her in a way that was valuable to her and proud, too, that she had trusted me so deeply so that it was possible for me to do so. The sense of satisfaction and fulfilment and the emotions I felt then are still with me, reminding me of the power and the richness of the experience for me.

I tell this story now as one that gives insights into the restorying of my understandings of collaboration and of collegial, professional relationships. The process of reliving and writing about the details of this incident gives me further insights into my own practice, and I am reminded of the ways in which my image of story and of relationships guides that practice. I am reminded also of the way in which I have storied the incident from my current position, as our attempt to tell a shared story within which students would tell stories of themselves through which they would learn and grow. I am reminded of the influence of Phyllis Rose (1983), whose words— "all living is a creative act of greater or lesser authenticity, hindered or helped by the fictions to which we submit ourselves" (p. 17)—caused me to think about the co-creation of shared plots within collaborative relationships, and of the highly personal, emotional, intellectual, physical, moral, and aesthetic process of doing so. I have come to understand the construction of these shared stories as the process of bringing our individual images together and projecting them forward toward a shared imaginative understanding for the future.

Research as Professional Development: Telling Stories, Changing Lives

The process of engaging in collaborative research provided Anne and me with a situation within which we each spoke with our own voice in order to hear the meanings we felt inside us as we thought about our teaching and learning and about our collaboration. We raised our voices to co-create a text for our collaborative practice, and I recorded the details of the stories we learned to live as we did so. Our stories record the details of the construction and reconstruction of our personal practical knowledge through practice and the reflection on practice and highlight the very personal, emotional, situational, and tentative ways in which we know and in which we learned to know. Anne's response to the written document was one of joy and pride, and I recorded her comments in my journal in March 1991. At this time the document was complete, and Anne was getting ready to retire at the end of her teaching career in June 1991. Her comments moved me very deeply, and I quote them here:

> I feel very privileged to have this document, which is a kind of tribute to my career as a teacher, and of which I feel very proud. I have always liked the way you have talked about teachers and acknowledged us as experienced and knowledgeable, which I believe we are. This kind of research presents "the teacher's voice," and both of our voices can be heard here. I hope that the work we have done together will be of help to other teachers as they develop professional partnerships and explore things together as we did.

Through my attempts to make meaning of Anne's story and of our collaboration, I have come to tell my own story in new ways and to gain new understandings of my own personal practical knowledge. In a study that has focused on change, learning, and teacher development, I am surprised and delighted by the extent to which I have changed myself; reconstructed my own understandings of teaching, learning, and professional relationships; and gained new insights into research as professional development. Through the collaborative research process, I have also come to new understandings about the power of stories to change lives and have experienced the way in which our shared story changed mine. With this came also new understandings of the importance and value of the creation of a literature of teacher stories and stories of teacher development, where through the telling of our stories we can create landscapes for ourselves and our colleagues to live in, within which to imagine new possibilities and to give voice and life to stories of their own.

Our relationship had many acknowledged benefits for each of us, yet we also recognized that it was complicated because of its dual nature, that of being simultaneously a teacher-consultant relationship and a participant-researcher relationship that was being documented and would eventually be made public. The trust and respect necessary for the establishment of the former relationship became critical for the continuance of the latter, where matters were being written about and made public and which Anne described as a disadvantage she felt. The anxiety and discomfort she felt at the thought of being written about was only alleviated when she learned through lived experiences that she could be open, trusting, and vulnerable without risk of being betrayed. The way that those lived experiences were felt can best be described by Anne's explanation of being a participant in collaborative research in this next piece. Her words bring insights to the meaning of research as professional development, and I have drawn from my field notes of October 1989, written after a seminar where I presented the research to my colleagues at OISE, and which Anne attended.

Learning to Trust and Trusting to Learn

You have proven to me many times that I could really trust you. I learned that I could do this early on when you gave me things to read as you were writing them. This was very important to me, as I realized then that I would have a say in what was written and the way in which it was written. The experience of seeing things on paper was always a shock, as somehow things look different on paper and it is especially critical that the meaning be exactly right. I would worry that an inadvertent comment would hurt somebody's feelings, so it was really important that we worked together to make sure that the intended meanings came out and that we chose the exact words to express them. When we did this, I knew that I could trust you and also that my privacy would be respected.

I came to realize how important all this was to me when there was a situation early on where I pointed out that some small things were not right from my point of view in something you had written. We talked and changed the words so that they fit my way of understanding, and they were only small details but they were very important to me because they were about kids, so they had to be just right. Another incident like this concerned some personal details that I was uncomfortable with making public, and when I told you about this, you had no problem with taking these out altogether, so I felt that I could talk openly and freely with you and that I would have control over things in this way. This all makes a big difference and increases the level of trust, the willingness to take risks and the comfort with being written about, if that is ever possible! I tell you things that I have not told to anyone else, and I talk about other people in my life quite openly, knowing that you respect my privacy and that we understand each other.

   Being talked about and being written about is hard for me, and the seminar I attended where you presented the research was an embarrassing experience for me. I felt centered out and the focus of attention, and of course I hate to be in the spotlight. Looking back on it now, though, I think that it wasn't so bad really, and if you asked me to, I would do it all again because it would help you and that's what friends are for.... I think that we were a great team. We worked together in a way that I never thought I would have again, playing off each other and also playing together right from the start.

CHAPTER 8

Reflections

ON TEACHING, LEARNING, AND INQUIRY

For as long as I can remember,
I have noticed sounds.
The crow's harsh caw.
The soft squelch of boggy ground
And the songs inside stones.

They became the soundscapes of a mind,
Shaped by stories and by stone,
Grey wind-swept limestone.
In circles rippling back in time,
They are ancient texts that have marked my soul.

"Don't go near those bogs" they said,
"Those bottomless holes will suck you down
And you'll never be heard of again."

I skirt the soft and springy moss,
The small brown pools and ferny ways.
Searching for stone-full voice and sound
And heard as if for the first time now,
Echoing the music of the marrow-bone.

Mary Beattie, "Touchstone," November 1990

Constructing and Reconstructing Stories of Professionalism

The writing of this the final chapter presupposes an ending. Within the endings of the temporal stories told throughout the chapters written here have lain the seeds of many new beginnings and the start of new circles within the spirals of the narratives of those whose stories they have told. In telling our stories, Anne and I have explored times in each of our lives when we have experienced change and have attempted to make mean-

139

ing of what we were experiencing in the light of the pasts that shaped us and the futures we imagined as they extended out of those pasts. We have each told of the meaning of the changes we have experienced, forging them from the ways in which the theories and practices of our lives have interacted and shaped each other.

Many voices can be heard throughout these chapters, our own voices and the voices of those who have influenced us within the cultural and sociopolitical environments in which we live; the voices from the past and those of the future, linked to give purpose and direction to our daily lives and to help us to make meaning of our experiences. The telling of our stories took place concurrent with the living and the retelling and within the ongoing attempt to make sense of life's experiences through the narrative unity of our lives as we have already lived them. It was during the process of writing that I came to understand that these stories of change focusing on learning, growth, and professional development are all fundamentally about voice—the discovery and rediscovery of voice, the development of increased capacities to listen to one's own voice and the voices of others, and the expression of self through practice and writing. It was through the writing that I have come to see that it is through the telling and retelling of our stories of practice that we construct and reconstruct our understandings of who we are, can create new and more significant versions of ourselves, and can thus transform ourselves. Through our stories, we hope that others will hear the sounds and the reverberations of their own voices and will be inspired to tell and to retell the stories of their lives also.

The process of inquiry through practice and of the writing about that practice is one of listening in and of reaching out, of continuously centering and stretching, and of constructing and reconstructing more authentic meanings for our lives. During a time of change, this process takes place under conditions that disturb the balance, the harmonies, and the relational modes of interacting that we know, and it requires us to make new configurations, constructions, and compositions to fulfil our changed needs. Concurrent with my attempts to write Anne's story in Chapters 5 and 6, I was involved in a similar situation in my own life to the one I was describing and experiencing the change from being a consultant to being a teacher of teachers in a faculty of education. As I wrote, I was feeling the gap between the told and the lived story in my daily life, the sense of being "out of step with the march of surrounding things" and searching for the equilibrium and the harmony I had known. The experience of writing Anne's story and of my growing understandings of the meanings of her experiences was a valuable and educative one for me. The writing was providing me with stories to live in as I struggled to make sense of my own story and with a framework within which to begin to reconstruct the present I was living and the future I was stretching toward, so that they could become a part of a new and different whole. Through the process of the creation of forms and language within which a reader could live vicariously and could understand the meaning of the experience of change, I was providing myself with stories that were informing my own developing story and helping me to bring a new shape and form to my own professional life. Linking my own image and imagination together, I could begin to construct a scenario of the mind where, as the principal actor in the piece, I could imagine and construct a new professional story within which I would create new forms and relations in order to adapt to my new environment. Through stories and with stories, life and research supported and enhanced each other, giving and receiving and reminding me again of the centrality and interconnectedness of story in my research, my teaching, and my life.

Through the writing, I have continually explored the relationships I feel between my own developing voice and those voices that have influenced me, that have interacted with mine and have helped me to become more than I am—the voices of colleagues, of friends, and of the writers whose work speaks to me. It was through the writing that I learned that the process itself was one of finding my own voice and of locating myself within the stories and the music that have shaped that voice and influenced its sounds and rhythms. At the end of that process, I reread Crites (1971) and heard him in a new way, knowing now that he was describing the feelings that I have felt, the experience I have lived, and helping me to explain me to myself.

> The music of a people, or even a cohesive group, is peculiarly its own. It is a particular musical style that permits a group's life style, its incipient musicality, to express itself in full dance and song. The connection is of course reciprocal: The musical style in turn molds the life style. But it cannot be an altogether alien mold. There is a beautiful paradox in the peculiar intensity with which a person responds to music which is "his own": Even if he has not heard it before it is familiar, as though something is sounding in it that he has always felt in his bones; and yet it is really new. It is his own style, revealed to him at an otherwise unimaginable level of clarity and intensity. (p. 294)

The process of exploring the voices that have influenced me and of hearing my own developing voice caused me to focus my attentions on the differences between the lived and the told story of my life. I recognized the necessity for the retelling and the power of the writing to help me to examine that story which was changing as I wrote it, due in so many ways to the educative and aesthetic qualities of the process of writing itself for me. The writing, conversations about writing, and reading what others have said about the process have helped me to further understand my long-standing fear and love–hate relationship with expressive writing, a story I have written about in the Prologue. Eisner (1991) has helped me to come to new understandings of my changing relationship with this kind of writing and of the profound satisfactions I am finding in the doing of it, casting a new light on what I was coming to know from my experience, and causing me to begin to make the connections between the aesthetic in art, in writing, in science, in the practical life, and in my own life.

Through the writing I have come to understand the concept of control in new ways and to see that in the conferring of order to ideas through form, the tension between creativity and control is maintained in a balanced relationship. I have come to understand major change as the struggle to find a new center from which to hear the sounds of one's own voice and the voices of others who are stakeholders in the educational process, to make meanings of those voices in circumstances that are often found to be what T. S. Eliot (1944) termed "unpropitious," and to cocreate new maxims, new customs, and new standards.

I have come to understand power as being able to tell one's own story and empowering others to find their voices and to tell their stories also. To have control and personal power is to have options regarding ways to think, to imagine, and to be, and choices among stories to live in. I have come to understand my interest in curriculum implementation as an issue of form, and to see it within my ongoing struggle with the balance between autonomous creativity and disciplined control, be it in life, in writing, or in teaching. I acknowledge that this particular struggle will always be with me.

For both Anne and me, the process of inquiry was a process of finding a new center, of the rediscovery of voice and the sounding of those voices to help others to discover their own voices. In each of our stories there was a move away from fragmentation toward greater unity, harmony, and wholeness; a focus on new relations and connections between the relations already existing in the environment; and the desire and the will to engage in further inquiry due to the deep satisfactions that emanated from the creation of new forms and the restoration of order and harmony in our lives. For two teachers, one at the end of her career and one in midcareer, the process in each case revealed patterns necessitating the continual telling, living, and retelling of the stories of ourselves in our ongoing exploration of who we are as teachers and learners.

The process of writing Anne's story animated the retelling of my own story, and as I wrote about the aesthetic qualities of her inquiry, which brought her a new sense of professionalism, greater capacities for growth and change, and a sense of renewal, I, too, was experiencing the aesthetic qualities of what I was creating. My situation was again one of "finding the music" and of experiencing it as the discovery of a coherence, a harmony, and a unity in my life that had somehow been incomplete until the untold stories were revealed and fastened through words into stories, poems, descriptions, and explanations. Through the writing I have learned about myself as a person, a teacher, a researcher, and a writer, and I have come to new understandings of the connections among them. I can now see the ways in which they interact and inform one another, influencing and changing one another in the process as the energies of each are harnessed in the service of the other, and new possibilities, relations, and forms are created.

The Making of Relations: Changing, Learning, and Growing

> O chestnut tree, great-rooted blossomer,
> Are you the leaf, the blossom or the bole?
> O body swayed to music, O brightening glance,
> How can we know the dancer from the dance?
> (Yeats, 1961, "Among School Children," p. 245)

To change the way in which we think requires that we make new forms, new relations and connections, and transform what we know by building a reconstructed personal world within which we live out a new and transformed story of ourselves. The personal and the professional are linked in inextricable ways, and the process of constructing and reconstructing personal practical knowledge is bounded only by birth and death and by the beginnings, middles, and endings that we ourselves impose upon the experiences we have between them. We construct our systems of coherence in ways that link our realities to our embodied imaginative understandings, and we do so in ways that are as private as they are personal and as potent as they are powerful to us both as individuals and as members of communities. Our purposes have their origins within the ongoing awareness of the changing reality within and around us, and they take their cues, rhythms, directions, and the impetus for the telling and retelling of our stories from those realities.

In our decisions to become teachers and educational researchers, we create situations in which the necessity for continuous learning and professional growth, and the telling and retelling of our stories, is a fundamental aspect of that professionalism. The stories we live out in our classrooms and in our research are intertwined with the stories of students, of colleagues, of administrators, and of policy makers, and our professionalism calls for us to be authentic and accountable not only to ourselves but also to those whose narratives are linked to ours within this environment. This professionalism and authenticity of practice requires that we listen, hear, and respond to the stories of others as we engage in the co-creation of shared meanings, and that we be true to ourselves and to those with whom we are in relation within our professional communities. Becoming increasingly more true to ourselves and to others within our communities is old advice and as valuable today as when it was first given by Polonius to his son Laertes:

> This above all: to thine own self be true,
> And it must follow as the night the day,
> Thou canst not then be false to any man.
>
> *Hamlet*, I, iii, 78–80

Thus the art of teaching and of research requires that we be true to our own voices and to the voices of those with whom we are connected within our professional settings, informed by both but surrendering to neither, and that we live out the well-made music of responsible and enlightened practice in our classrooms and in our research situations.

I have come to believe that at the heart of meaningful educational reform and change lie the narratives and the interaction of narratives of those who live out their lives in educational settings. Within our current educational situations, where the fabric of daily life for teachers and students alike is comprised of continual movement and change, it is necessary for life experiences to be reflected upon in order to continually re-create our understandings of the lives we live and the contexts within which we live them. Collaboration, collegiality, and conversation provide us with the means with which to interact, to exchange ideas and understandings, and to construct new and more significant meanings for our lives within the context of the narrative unity of those lives. It becomes clear how externally imposed changes can only be superficial at best, in that they fail to connect with the world as it is understood and lived, and are limiting in their ability to influence or direct the ways in which future stories of teaching and learning are imagined and lived out. Collaboration, collegiality, and conversation provide us with the means for reform and professional change within the context of self and community.

It is very significant to me that as I write the final chapter of this book, I do so at a time when changes of great magnitude, previously unimagined, have recently taken place throughout the world, and their impact is already being felt in many areas of our daily lives. The countries of Eastern Europe are restructuring themselves politically, socially, and economically; the ideological boundaries that have long separated East and West are coming to the fore; and interaction, discourse, stories, and listening and responding to others seem more critical at a time like this than they have ever seemed. Within this context, Mary Robinson (1990), Ireland's first woman president, said in her inauguration address to the nation:

> As the person chosen by you to symbolise this Republic and to project our self image to others, I will seek to encourage mutual understanding and tolerance between all the different communities sharing this island.
>
> In seeking to do this I shall rely to a large extent on symbols. But symbols are what unite and divide people. Symbols give us our identity, our self image, our way of explaining ourselves to ourselves and to others. Symbols in turn determine the kinds of stories we tell; and the stories we tell determine the kind of history we make and remake. I want Áras an Uachtaráin [the president's residence] to be a place where people can tell diverse stories—in the knowledge that there is someone there to listen.
>
> I want this Presidency to promote the telling of stories—stories of celebration through the arts and stories of conscience and of social justice. As a woman, I want women who have felt themselves outside history to be written back into history, in the words of Evan Boland, "finding a voice where they found a vision".
>
> May God direct me so that my Presidency is one of justice, peace and love. May I have the fortune to preside over an Ireland at a time of exciting transformation when we enter a new Europe where old wounds can be healed, a time when, in the words of Seamus Heaney "hope and history rhyme". (p. 15)

Through the stories we hear, tell, and live, we bring our hopes and our histories together, and through them we reflect on our lives, imagining new possibilities and framing the ongoing imbalances, dilemmas, joys, and successes we have within the context of the unity of new life stories. As Johnson (1987) explains: "Not only are we born into complex communal narratives, we also experience, understand, and order our lives as stories that we are living out. Whatever human rationality consists in, it is certainly tied up with narrative structure and the quest for narrative unity" (p. 172). Through the telling and retelling of our stories of experience, we come to know ourselves and our changing environments and to transform both self and environment. The process can be a difficult and painful one requiring introspection and self-exposure, yet those of us who engage in it do so in order to gain increased understandings of ourselves within the context of self and of relationship, of community and of society. We do so, too, to provide others with stories within which they can live and by which they can begin to find voices to tell their own stories and to gain new understandings and control of their own lives.

It seems safe to predict that we will always live in classrooms, schools, universities, communities, societies, and a world where others hold views, values, and beliefs different from ours. The process of working through our differences and of moving toward shared understandings lies in interaction and in the reciprocal telling and valuing of our own and each other's stories. Change and growth take place as practitioners and researchers continue to work together, voicing understandings, entering into the understandings of others, and engaging in the mutual adaptation and continual reconstruction of self in relation to both self and community. Such collaborations and interactions are necessary for the ongoing reconciliation of conflicting and clashing views and for continual movement toward shared understandings and co-created customs and standards for self and for community. The sounds of dialogue, debate, and discussion, and of conflict, controversy, and conversation are the sounds of the interaction of narratives, of lives meeting lives, and of the making of new relations, new principles, and new meanings for self and for others. They are the sounds of personal change, professional change, and of social change. Reform, therefore, can be imagined, not as the monologic imposition of ideas, beliefs, and values by one person or group on another, but as the polyphonic re-forming and reconstruction of understandings by all the parties involved through the interaction of narratives.

In the telling and retelling of our stories, we change, we learn, and we grow, giving up the stories of ourselves that we hold when we can replace them with richer and more significant versions more suited to our current environments and to the future we foresee. Through narrative inquiry where our individual narratives interact, we collaborate in the telling and retelling of stories of the past and in the co-creation of stories for the present and the future. When our collective images and imaginations are linked in the creative act of giving voice to shared visions, the process can enable and empower us to re-form and transform ourselves and our communities.

REFERENCES

Banville, J. (1976). *Dr. Copernicus.* London: Secker and Warburg.

Banville, J. (1981). *Kepler.* London: Secker and Warburg.

Banville, J. (1989). *The book of evidence.* London: Secker and Warburg.

Barnes, J. (1984). *Flaubert's parrot.* London: Picador, Pan Books.

Barnes, J. (1989). *A history of the world in 10 and a half chapters.* New York: Knopf.

Bateson, M. C. (1989). *Composing a life.* New York: Atlantic Monthly Press.

Beattie, M. (1993, September). Teachers. *Journal of Among Teachers Community, 20.*

Burns, R. (1982, October). *Conceptualizing the process of teaching: A review of the literature.* Paper presented at the General Assembly Meeting, International Association for the Evaluation of Educational Achievement, Toronto.

Callaghan, B. (1978). *The Hogg poems and drawings.* Don Mills, Ontario: General Publishing.

Callaghan, B. (1989). *The way the angel spreads her wings.* Toronto: Lester and Orpen Dennys.

Carr, D. (1986). *Time, history and narrative.* Indianapolis: Indiana University Press.

Casto, R. (1980). *The arrivals.* Toronto: Studio Press.

Cicourel, A. V. (1964). *Method and measurement in sociology.* New York: Free Press of Glencoe.

Clandinin, D. J. (1983). *A conceptualization of image as a component of teachers' personal practical knowledge.* Unpublished doctoral dissertation, University of Toronto.

Clandinin, D. J. (1986). *Classroom practice: Teacher images in action.* London: Falmer.

Clandinin, D. J. (1993). *Learning to teach, teaching to learn: Stories of collaboration in teacher education.* New York: Teachers College Press.

Clandinin, D. J., & Connelly, F. M. (1986a). Rhythms in teaching: The narrative study of teachers' personal practical knowledge of classrooms. *Teaching and teacher education, 2*(4), 377–387.

Clandinin, D. J., & Connelly, F. M. (1986b). The reflective practitioner and practitioner's narrative unities. *Canadian Journal of Education, 11*(2), 184–198.

Clandinin, D. J., & Connelly, F. M. (1987). Teachers' personal knowledge: What counts as "personal" in studies of the personal. *Journal of Curriculum Studies, 19*(6), 487–500.

Clandinin, D. J., & Connelly, F. M. (1991). Narrative and story in practice and research. In D. Schön (Ed.), *The reflective turn: Case studies in and of educational practice* (pp. 258–281). New York: Teachers College Press.

Clandinin, D. J., & Connelly, F. M. (1992). The teacher as curriculum-maker. In P. W. Jackson (Ed.), *Handbook of research on curriculum, a project of the American Educational Research Association* (pp. 363–401). New York: Macmillan.

Clark, C. M., & Peterson, P. L. (1986). Teachers' thought processes. In M. C. Wittrock (Ed.), *Handbook of research on teaching* (3rd ed.; pp. 255–296). New York: Macmillan.

Clark, C. M., & Yinger, R. J. (1977). Research on teacher thinking. *Curriculum Inquiry, 7*(4), 279–304.

Cole, A. (1987). *Teachers' spontaneous adaptations: A mutual interpretation.* Unpublished doctoral dissertation, University of Toronto.

Coleridge, S. (1974). Samuel Taylor Coleridge (1772–1834). In M. H. Abrams (Ed.), *The Norton anthology of English literature* (3rd ed.; Vol. 2, pp. 283–365). New York: W. W. Norton.

Coles, R. (1989). *The call of stories: Teaching and the moral imagination.* Boston: Houghton Mifflin.

Connelly, F. M., & Clandinin, D. J. (1986). On narrative method, personal philosophy, and narrative unities in the story of teaching. *Journal of Research in Science Teaching, 23*(4), 292–310.

Connelly, F. M., & Clandinin, D. J. (1988). *Teachers as curriculum planners: Narratives of experience.* New York: Teachers College Press.

Connelly, F. M., & Clandinin, D. J. (1990). Stories of experience and narrative inquiry. *Educational Researcher, 19*(5), 2–14.

Connelly, F. M., & Clandinin, D. J. (1991). Narrative inquiry: Storied experience. In E. C. Short (Ed.), *Forms of curriculum inquiry: Guidelines for the conduct of educational research* (pp. 121–154). Albany, NY: State University of New York Press.

Connelly, F. M., & Clandinin, D. J. (1993). Reflective practice: Thoughts from the community. *Orbit, 23* (4), 1.

Connelly, F. M., & Clandinin, D. J. (1994). Telling teaching stories. *Teacher Education Quarterly, 21*(2), 145–158.

Cooper-Clark, D. (1983). *Designs of darkness.* Bowling Green, OH: Bowling Green University Press.

Cooper-Clark, D. (1986). *Interviews with contemporary novelists* (Vol. 1). London: Macmillan.

Crites, S. (1971). The narrative quality of experience. *Journal of the American Academy of Religion, 39*(3), 291–311.

Crites, S. (1979). The aesthetics of self deception. *Soundings, 62,* 107–129.

Dewey, J. (1916). *Democracy in education.* New York: Macmillan.

Dewey, J. (1934). *Art as experience.* New York: Capricorn Books.

Dwyer, K. (1979). The dialogic of ethnology. *Dialectical Anthropology, 4,* 205–224.

Eisner, E. W. (1985a). Aesthetic modes of knowing. In E. W. Eisner (Ed.), *Learning and teaching the ways of knowing* (84th yearbook of the National Society for the Study of Education, Part II., pp. 23–36). Chicago: University of Chicago Press.

Eisner, E. W. (1985b). *The educational imagination* (2nd ed.). New York: Macmillan.

Eisner, E. W. (1988). The primacy of experience and the politics of method. *Educational Researcher, 17*(5), 15–20.

Eisner, E. W. (1991). *The enlightened eye: On doing qualitative research.* New York: Macmillan.

Elbaz, F. (1983). *Teacher thinking: A study of practical knowledge.* London: Croom Helm.

Eliot, T. S. (1944). *Four quartets.* London: Faber and Faber.

Enns-Connolly, E. (1985). *Translation as interpretative act: A narrative study of translation in university-level foreign language teaching.* Unpublished doctoral dissertation, University of Toronto.

Fleming, T., & Craig, M. (1990). The anatomy of a resignation: Margaret Strong and the New Westminster School Board, 1913-1915. *Journal of Educational Administration and Foundations, 5,* 7-23.

Fleming, T., Smyly, C., & White, J. (1990). "Beyond hope and redemption": Lottie Bowron and the rural school teachers of British Columbia, 1928-1934. *Journal of Educational Administration and Foundations, 5*(2), 7-53.

Frye, N. (1963). *The educated imagination.* Toronto: Canadian Broadcasting Company.

Fullan, M. (1982). *The meaning of educational change.* Toronto: Ontario Institute for Studies in Education Press and Teachers College Press.

Fullan, M. (1991). *The new meaning of educational change* (2nd ed.). New York: Teachers College Press.

Geertz, C. (1983). *Local knowledge.* New York: Basic Books.

Gilligan, C. (1982). *In a different voice.* Cambridge, MA: Harvard University Press.

Graves, R. (1975). *Collected poems 1975.* London: Cassell & Co.

Guba, E., & Lincoln, Y. (1985). *Naturalistic inquiry.* Beverly Hills, CA: Sage.

Hardy, B. (1968). Towards a poetics of fiction: An approach through narrative. *Novel, 2,* 5-14.

Hardy, B. (1975). *Tellers and listeners: The narrative imagination.* London: Athlone Press.

Heaney, S. (1980). *Preoccupations: Selected prose 1968-1978.* London: Faber and Faber.

Heaney, S. (1984). *Station Island.* London: Faber and Faber.

Heaney, S. (1987). *The haw lantern.* London: Faber and Faber.

Heaney, S. (1988). *The government of the tongue: The 1986 T. S. Eliot Memorial Lectures and other critical writings.* London: Faber and Faber.

Heaney, S. (1989, October 27-November 2). Two poems by Seamus Heaney: "A Latch," "A Window." *Times Literary Supplement, 4517,* 1172.

Heidegger, M. (1962). *Being and time* (J. Macquarrie & E. Robinson, Trans.). New York: Harper & Row.

Heilbrun, C. (1988). *Writing a woman's life.* New York: Ballantine.

Hunt, D. E. (1976). Teachers are psychologists too: On the application of psychology to education. *Canadian Psychological Review, 17,* 210-218.

Hunt, D. E. (1979). The new three R's in person-environment interaction: Responsiveness, reciprocality and reflexivity. *Dutch Journal of Educational Research, 4,* 184-190.

Hunt, D. E. (1980). *Studies in mutual adaptation* (Progress Report No. 4). Toronto: Ontario Institute for Studies in Education.

Hunt, D. E. (1985, February). Demystifying learning style. *Orbit, 73,* 1-4.

Hunt, D. E. (1986). Teachers' adaptation: "Reading" and "flexing" to students. *Journal of Teacher Education, 27,* 268-275.

Hunt, D. E. (1987). *Beginning with ourselves in theory, practice and human affairs.* Cambridge, MA: Brookline Books; Toronto: Ontario Institute for Studies in Education Press.

Hunt, D. E., & Gow, J. (1984). How to be your own best theorist II. *Theory into Practice, 118,* 64-71.

Husserl, E. (1970). *The crisis of European sciences and transcendental phenomenology* (D. Carr,

Trans.). Evanston, IL: Northwestern University Press. (Original work published 1954)

Jackson, P. (1966). The way teaching is. In O. Sand & L. J. Bishop (Eds.), *The way teaching is: Report on the seminar on teaching* (pp. 7-27). Washington, DC: Association for Supervision and Curriculum Development/National Education Association, Centre for the Study of Instruction.

Jackson, P. W. (1990a, October). The functions of educational research. *Educational Researcher, 19*(7), 3-9.

Jackson, P. W. (1990b). *Life in classrooms* (reissued ed.). New York: Teachers College Press.

James, W. (1975). *The meaning of truth.* Cambridge, MA: Harvard University Press. (Original work published 1909)

Janesick, V. (1982). Of snakes and circles: Making sense of classroom group processes through a case study. *Curriculum Inquiry, 12*(2), 161-190.

Johnson, M. (Ed.). (1981). *Philosophical perspectives on metaphor.* Minneapolis: University of Minnesota Press.

Johnson, M. (1987). *The body in the mind: The bodily basis of meaning, imagination and reason.* Chicago: University of Chicago Press.

Johnson, M. (1989). Embodied knowledge. *Curriculum Inquiry, 19*(4), 361-377.

Joyce, J. (1964). *Portrait of the artist as a young man.* New York: Viking Press. (Original work published 1922)

Kavanagh, P. (1986). Patrick Kavanagh. In P. Muldoon (Ed.), *The Faber book of contemporary Irish poetry.* London: Faber and Faber.

Kermode, F. (1967). *The sense of an ending: Studies in the theory of fiction.* New York: Oxford University Press.

Kidder, T. (1989). *Among schoolchildren.* Boston: Houghton Mifflin.

Kinsella, T. (1970). *Notes from the land of the dead and other poems.* New York: Knopf.

Kroma, S. (1983). *Personal practical knowledge of language in teaching.* Unpublished doctoral dissertation, University of Toronto.

Kundera, M. (1976). *The farewell party.* New York: Penguin.

Kundera, M. (1978). *The book of laughter and forgetting.* New York: Harper Collins.

Kundera, M. (1984). *The unbearable lightness of being.* New York: Harper & Row.

Kundera, M. (1986). *Life is elsewhere.* New York: Penguin.

Kundera, M. (1988). *The art of the novel.* New York: Harper & Row.

LaRocque, L., & Oberg, A. A. (1980, June). *Implications of research on teacher decision-making for future research, teacher education, and curriculum making.* Paper presented at the annual meeting of the Canadian Association for Curriculum Studies, Montreal.

Langer, S. (1957). *Problems of art.* New York: Scribner.

Lincoln, Y. S., & Guba, E. G. (1985). *Naturalistic inquiry.* Beverly Hills, CA: Sage.

Lively, P. (1984). *According to Mark.* London and New York: Penguin.

Lively, P. (1988). *Moontiger.* London: Penguin.

MacIntyre, A. (1966). *A short history of ethics.* New York: MacMillan.

MacIntyre, A. (1981). *After virtue: A study in moral theory.* London: Gerald Duckworth.

Marris, P. (1974). *Loss and change.* London: Routledge and Kegan Paul.

McGahern, J. (1965). *The dark.* London: Faber and Faber.

McGahern, J. (1985). *High ground.* London: Faber and Faber.

McGahern, J. (1990). *Among women*. London: Faber and Faber.

McKeon, R. (1952). Philosophy and action. *Ethics, 62*(2), 79–100.

Mink, L. O. (1978). Narrative form as a cognitive instrument. In R. H. Canary & H. Kozicki (Eds.), *The writing of history* (pp. 129–149). Madison: University of Wisconsin Press.

Montague, J. (1972). *The rough field.* Dublin: Dolmen Press.

Munby, H. (1986). Metaphor in the thinking of teachers: An exploratory study. *Journal of Curriculum Studies, 18,* 197–209.

Newman, P. C. (1990, June 22). The past and presentation. *The Globe and Mail,* p. A12.

Noddings, N. (1986). Fidelity in teaching, teacher education, and research for teaching. *Harvard Educational Review, 56*(4), 496–510.

Paley, V. G. (1981). *Wally's stories: Conversations in the kindergarten.* Cambridge, MA: Harvard University Press.

Paley, V. G. (1986). *Molly is three: Growing up in school.* Chicago: University of Chicago Press.

Peshkin, A. (1985). Virtuous subjectivity: In the participant observer's I's. In D. Berg & K. K. Smith (Eds.), *Exploring clinical methods for sound research* (pp. 267–281). Beverly Hills, CA: Sage.

Polanyi, M. (1958). *Personal knowledge.* Chicago: University of Chicago Press.

Polkinghorne, D. E. (1988). *Narrative knowing and the human sciences.* Albany: State University of New York Press.

Reid, W. A. (1988). Institutions and practices: Professional education reports and the language of reform. *Educational Researcher, 17,* 10–15.

Ricoeur, P. (1984). *Time and narrative* (Vol. 1). Chicago: University of Chicago Press.

Ricoeur, P. (1985). *Time and narrative* (Vol. 2). Chicago: University of Chicago Press.

Ricoeur, P. (1988). *Time and narrative* (Vol. 3). Chicago: University of Chicago Press.

Robinson, M. (1990, December 4). Inaugural address to the nation. *Irish Independent,* p. 15.

Rose, P. (1983). *Parallel lives.* New York: Vintage Books.

Rosen, H. (1986, March). The importance of story. *Language Arts, 63*(3), 226–237.

Scholes, R., & Kellogg, R. (1966). *The nature of narrative.* New York: Oxford University Press.

Schön, D. (1983). *The reflective practitioner: How professionals think in action.* New York: Basic Books.

Schön, D. (1987). *Educating the reflective practitioner.* San Francisco and London: Jossey-Bass.

Schulman, L. S. (1987). Knowledge and teaching: Foundations of the new reform. *Harvard Educational Review, 57*(1), 1–22.

Schutz, A., & Luckman, T. (1973). *The structures of the life-world.* Evanston, IL: Northwestern University Press.

Schwab, J. (1971). The practical: Arts of eclectic. *School Review, 79,* 493–542.

Schwab, J. (1983). The practical 4: Something for curriculum professors to do. *Curriculum Inquiry, 13*(3), 239–265.

Shakespeare, W. (1978). *The annotated Shakespeare* (Vol. 1; A. L. Rowse, Ed.). New York: Clarkson N. Potter.

Sims, N. (Ed.). (1984). *The literary journalists*. New York: Ballantine Books.

Skeat, W. (Ed.). (1983). *A concise etymological dictionary of the English language*. Oxford: Oxford University Press.

Solzhenitsyn, A. (1973). *The Gulag Archipelago*. New York: Harper & Row.

Spence, D. P. (1982). *Narrative truth and historical method*. New York: Norton.

Stenhouse, L. (1975). *An introduction to curriculum research and development*. London: Heinemann.

Tennyson, A. (1894). *The complete works of Alfred Lord Tennyson*. London: E. H. Wells.

White, H. (1973). *Metahistory*. Baltimore, MD: Johns Hopkins University Press.

Wordsworth, W. (1974). William Wordsworth (1770–1859). In M. H. Abrams (Ed.), *The Norton anthology of English literature* (3rd ed.; Vol. 2 , pp. 111–267). New York: Norton.

Yeats, W. B. (1961). *Collected poems of W. B. Yeats*. London: Macmillan.

INDEX

ABOUT THE AUTHOR

Mary Beattie is an assistant professor of education at the University of Toronto. She holds a doctorate degree in education from the University of Toronto and master's degrees in English (York University, Ontario) and in education (University of Toronto). She has taught for 17 years at the elementary and intermediate levels in the public school systems in Canada, England, and Ireland. She has also worked with experienced teachers as a consultant of curriculum and staff development with the board of education in which she taught in Toronto, Canada. Her ongoing research and writings focus on teachers' knowledge, professional development, and narrative inquiry.